Norm

By
Mark T. Sternhagen

Normal for Me, 2nd edition
Rev. 1c

Copyright 2016 by Mark T. Sternhagen
Publisher, CNSS Inc.
www.normal4me.com
cnssone@yahoo.com

ISBN: 978-1-68419-827-6

Dedicated to the Memory
of my cousin
Rita Marie Bickett-Spyksma

Her inspiration and connections because of her
made this book possible

Also I would like to thank all those who supported me along
the way, both in writing this book and in general. Most
importantly my parents, William J. and Mary Ruth
Sternhagen, they made some tough choices along the way.
Many I was not happy with at the time, but in the end they
were the right choices.

Forward

I never thought I was anything special. As I went through my life, it was all just normal for me—to wake up every morning, get dressed, put my braces on, grab my crutches to stand up and get out of bed, then go about my day, doing what I needed to get by. When I walked with my crutches, it was normal for me to be careful where I placed each crutch and each foot, or I would be on the ground. I never thought about inspiring anyone or anything like that, I just did what I had to in life to get by. Each of us, every one of us, has challenges, things that are hard for us. How we deal with them, live with them, and overcome them is what is really important. Sometimes we don't, sometimes we fall, but as long as every time we fall we get back up and go on, that is a success. I fell almost every day of my life up until sometime in my teenage years, but yet every time I did what was normal for me—I grabbed my crutches and pushed my way back up.

What is Polio? This description is taken from *Polio, an American Story* by David Oshinsky:

> Polio is an intestinal infection that spreads from person to person through direct contact, such as, unwashed hands, shared objects etc. Originally described in Greek and Roman literature dating back to about 1500BC, polio really started becoming widespread ironically with more modern attention focused on hygiene. Early outbreaks in the US were documented as early as 1894, with many localized epidemics thorough the 1950s, when the Salk killed virus vaccine was developed by Dr. Jonas Salk and his team, it was certified by the FDA in 1955. Polio is a very scary disease, when outbreaks would happen during the summer sometimes termed polio season. People would shut up their houses, keeping their children in doors. Swimming pools were closed, movie theaters, even

churches would close. Polio affects the motor neurons often destroying many of them. There are three basic strains of polio with a few variants within those. Type I is the most common of the three, the one most likely to lead to epidemics and paralysis of the limbs. Type II is a milder virus than type I, the likeliest to lead to asymptomatic cases, though it in the weak or unlucky it could still paralyze or kill. Type III is the rarest of all and that is a good thing, it is the one most likely to lead t o bulbar polio the infection of the medulla oblongata, leading to paralysis of the diaphragm, destruction of breathing and so often death. It starts out with flu like symptoms and in many cases it is little more than a very bad case of the flu. The worst cases can cause death with in a few hours. Many who contracted polio needed to be placed in an iron lung to help with breathing for an extended period of time. A few would be in an iron lung the rest of their lives. A significant percentage ended up with permanent disability, anything from a minor limp, to completely disabled. Normally it is localized in one or both legs. There are well documented cases of a number of children in single families dying from polio over a very short span of time. When children were bad or didn't wash up or something they were scolded with "do you want to spend the rest of your life in an iron lung?" Polio was the bogey man of the time. The Salk vaccine uses a killed virus system. It is not possible to contract polio from the Salk vaccine or from being around people that have been recently vaccinated with it.

The lasting effects from polio, such as those I have, come from attacks on the motor neurons that control the muscles, not the actual muscles themselves. The muscles eventually atrophy due lack of stimulation.

Normal for Me
By Mark T. Sternhagen
Chapter One

Back in 1956, when the Salk vaccine, that had been certified safe and affective for use in the US in 1955, became available in my home town of Scotland, South Dakota, my brothers and cousins were all vaccinated; however, I could not be because I was running a temp at the time, so it was contraindicated to vaccinate me. When the polio virus came around in August of 1957, all of us were likely exposed to it as we pretty much did everything together. The only one to get polio was me. I was diagnosed on August 5th, 1957. This was certainly a defining moment in my life. My family was, literally, the first in line when the vaccine came to Scotland. My Aunt Donna Orth was a registered nurse working with Dr. Jungman at the Scotland clinic, and knew how important it was to make sure her children, as well as her nephews and family members, were vaccinated.

My mom, Mary Sternhagen, was 24 and my dad Bill Jr. was 29. They had four small boys. Mike was three, Jim was two, I was 18 months, and John was barely 6 months old. I had actually learned to walk and climb at an early age. I was into everything! My folks had to keep the cupboard doors shut or I would crawl into them. They had to keep the kitchen chairs tied together under the table or I would be on top the table dancing, they had to take the handle off the front loading washing machine or I would climb in. I once even found the knob and tried to flush it down the toilet! It wasn't until my dad tried to fix the toilet that they found it. Just imagine what was going through the minds of my young parents when they were given the news that was so dreaded at that time. Their rambunctious son, Mark, had polio. For quite some time it was uncertain if I would even survive.

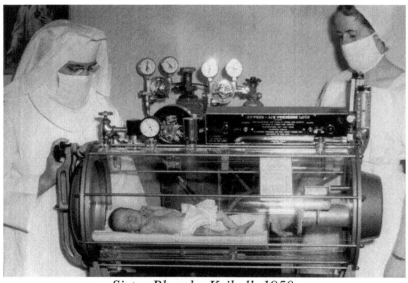

Sister Blanche Kribell, 1950,
Courtesy South Dakota Magazine

I don't remember a lot of what happened at that time. I was first taken to the Sacred Heart Hospital in Yankton, SD. My great aunt, Sister Blanche Kribell, was a registered nurse in obstetrics who had some experience dealing with polio patients. I remember little of what took place at that time, but how kindly she was shines through in my memory. As I understand from stories I heard along the way, she was the only one I would eat for. I am guessing my choice hinged on the fact she looked a lot like her sister, my grandmother Catherine Bickett. She was so nice and of course took a special interest in me. Sr. Blanche would, through the years, assist in some 30,000 deliveries and, because of her amazing memory, could relate stories about most of them. Because of her extensive work with young patients, she was inducted into the South Dakota Hall of Fame in 2003.

I was later moved to a polio ward at the Veterans Hospital in Omaha, NE. I was only one of about three children there at that time. The rest were adults. My only real recollection of my first time there involves a lot of pain. I later learned that was common with polio, as the muscles would contract against each other.

When I was first taken to Yankton, of course, my parents were in quite a state. My Uncle Tom once told me that was the only time he had ever seen my dad cry.

As I stated before, I was 18 months old at the time. My oldest brother Mike was three, Jim was two, and John was not yet one. This happened during the summer, and my Aunt Pat Bickett, who was 12 at the time, was staying with my family helping take care of us. Fortunately, when they took me to Yankton, she was there to stay with my brothers. My Grandmother Sternhagen had offered to take over care of me and my mom could concentrate on the other children. While it may have been a nice offer, luckily for me, my mom would hear nothing of that. I was her child and she was going to do what she could to take care of me. My grandmother was a bit put out. My folks asked that she and my grandfather Sternhagen go get the other boys and my Aunt Pat and take them to their house, also in Scotland. When my folks got back from Yankton later that evening, they still had not gotten around to picking up my brothers and Aunt Pat. I am sure my Grandmother Sternhagen had all the best intentions. I am quite confident that had my mom listened and agreed with Grandmother Sternhagen, my life would have turned out very differently, and not for the better.

My mom called her mom, my Grandma Bickett, who lived on a farm near Winfred, SD, about 75 miles away. Grandma and Grandpa jumped in the car, along with my Aunt Margaret, and made it to Scotland in an hour to help. Margaret stayed to help with the older boys, while Grandpa and Grandma returned to the farm, taking Aunt Pat and John with them.

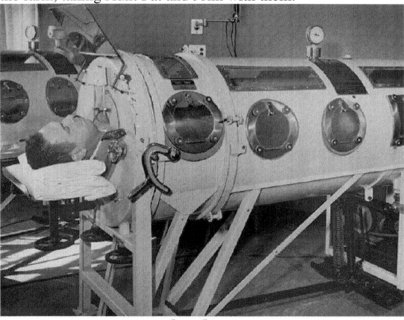

Iron Lung

My stay in the polio ward in Omaha lasted for more than a year. I spent my second birthday there. During part of the time, I was confined in an iron lung. Thankfully, I don't remember being in one, but I sure remember seeing others in them—some who would spend the rest of their lives in them.

I ended up back there a number of times for surgery, checkups, therapy, or new braces. One memory from that time really stands out. I was in the examination room and they told me to not be frightened, as I was going to have a lady doctor. That struck me as odd, because I never really differentiated the nurses, who were mostly female, from the doctors, who up to that point, were apparently male. To me, they were just people who were nice to me. Sometimes, in physical therapy, the therapists caused me some pain, but they were always nice about it, explaining the necessity.

One time I was back for a surgery on both legs, which meant casts and an extended stay. I remember some nurses, orderlies, and interns had a picnic, and they took me. I remember it was a lot of fun and, also, that they gave me the biggest hamburger I had ever seen. Another time, I remember some other patients in the room using coat hangers for an antenna on the TV, trying to receive All Star Wrestling. Years later, at CCHS (Crippled Children's Hospital and School), we would try something similar to receive that same show. Knowing All Star Wrestling, it was likely even the same episode.

Chapter 2

Growing up in Scotland, SD, we lived in a basement house. The idea was to eventually build an actual house, but start with the basement. It had concrete floors that got wet when it rained. I particularly remember one time when I was probably three years old. I was crawling at the time, since I couldn't walk due to the effects of polio. There was an apple under a table in the living room and, being a curious kid, I crawled over and took a bite. Use your science skills and think about what happens to an apple that sits for some time on wet concrete. It was quite rotten! I spit it out and blame that rotten apple for why, to this day, cannot stand to eat apples or most fresh fruit. I long ago gave up trying to convince myself that all fruit should not be judged by that one rotten apple.

Jim and Mike in the back, Mark in parka and John in front

All four of us boys slept in one room in the basement house. We eventually had two sets of bunk beds. At times, when the rains leaked in and wet floors, we'd use the ladders to go between the beds to keep our feet and knees dry. It was a challenge for me, but I did manage to make it a few times.

One year, for Christmas, we all got cowboy outfits with guns and holsters. We were riding the arms of the couch and a chair pretending they were our horses. If memory serves correctly, I was on one with my brother Jim in front. Mike got upset for some reason and threw his gun at us. Jim ducked and I got hit in the lip. This meant a trip to see my Aunt Donna, a wonderful person and a registered nurse. A couple of stitches later, I was back in the saddle! There was no ER back then, just my Aunt Donna at a small doctor's office in Scotland. That same year we also each got a Tonka truck, Mike got a pickup with a boat and trailer, so maybe that explains why he always liked boats and fishing later on? Jim got an allied van tractor trailer truck, John got a pickup with a horse trailer and I got a white garbage truck.

My mom used to do therapy with me when I was little. I would lay on back and she would do bicycles with me, pumping my legs as if I were riding a bicycle. She would always say things like "we are riding to Grandma's" or something like that. Mostly it was to keep my legs limber. Though I was supposed to push against her, I couldn't very well. I remember she really prompted me to push harder. I would try, partly because it seemed to me to make her sad when I did not. Of course, I didn't really understand how badly she wished I could push back more. She would also push in my ankles to bend them so my Achilles tendons wouldn't get too tight. This was kind of painful particularly on my left foot. I remember crying a lot. I also remember tears in her eyes and she kept going even when I cried. Funny thing though when she said we were bicycling to Grandma's house, I always envisioned it being my Grandma Sternhagen's and really wasn't all that interested in going there, though I never said that.

During my growing years, my best friend was our cocker spaniel, Sandy. He was always with us and very protective. Once, my brothers were hauling me around in the wagon and managed to dump me out. I was trying, with their help, to get back in the wagon. You have to realize we were probably all under five or six at the time. Some helpful citizen of Scotland came along and tried to help, but Sandy would have none of it. He growled and barked the warning, "Get away from my boys." My brothers did manage to get me back in the wagon and home. I understand the person who was attempting to "help" called my mother and gave her a tongue lashing for letting them haul around "that poor little crippled boy." Anyway, I survived that, along with many other such adventures. Sometimes a kid just has to be a kid.

Sandy was a great dog, and friend. He had one real problem though: for some reason he hated grocery delivery cars and their drivers. He always knew them on sight; even if they got a new car, he would know. I remember one time sitting outside playing by the house and one came by. The vehicles were usually station wagons for the ease of hauling the groceries and this one had the back window open to make the tail gate easy to drop. When he stopped at the stop sign by our house, Sandy took off, jumping in that open window and seconds later the grocery boy came running out the front door and the chase was on. As I recall, he ran to our house and in the front door. My mom came out and held Sandy so he could get back to his car and route.

Another 'Sandy' memory involves me trying to get him to pull me in the wagon. It seems as if we had read a story about sled dogs or mushing in the Alaskan frontier, in school. I found some rope, made a makeshift harness for him, hitched him up, and got in the wagon. He could not figure out what I wanted him to do. I kept saying, "Mush, Sandy, mush!" As soon as I said his name, he would come back to me in the wagon, until a grocery delivery car came by. I ended up with a quite a ride! Luckily, I wasn't very good at harness making. Sandy slipped loose after about 20 feet and took off after the delivery car. No amount of calling for him or yelling at him would stop him from giving chase. When he felt he had done his duty, he'd return to me.

My mom didn't drive, and since Scotland is a small town, she walked pretty much everywhere. Often, it was with me in tow in the wagon and, almost always, with Sandy walking along with us. Sandy was definitely a protective, one-family dog. When my mom would go into a store to shop, he would wait out front. Later, we found out that he would growl and bark to frighten people and keep them out of the store while my mom was inside.

I remember when they first opened the frosty shop in Scotland, it was a big day: free ice-cream cones for all! We all got our ice-cream cones, but realize it is very hard to walk on crutches and carry an ice-cream cone. I was doing my best, trying to get out of the way of others, when Sandy decided he needed to have some. Normally he would beg for food and normally it was ok, but when he jumped up on me, I was pretty unstable walking with one crutch, the other dangling (I used forearm type crutches and the cuffs would stay on your arm). When he jumped on me, I fell of course, dropping my ice-cream cone onto the sidewalk where he quickly made it disappear while I sat there crying. My oldest brother Mike went and asked if I could get another. At first they were reluctant, figuring we were just using an excuse to get another cone, but they finally gave in and I got my ice-cream.

When Sandy died, I had just gotten home for a vacation from CCHS and he wasn't around. Dad went out looking for him, and finally found him dead, lying in the middle of the street someplace, not a scratch on him, apparently from a heart attack. My guess is he was chasing a grocery delivery car and finally caught it just as he had a heart attack.

When I started school, kindergarten was in a different building, just south of the grade school. I believe it was an old lodge or country school building that had been moved in. Most public places were not "handicapped accessible."

There were steps to enter, but by that time, I was walking with a full left leg brace and right ankle brace. With the use of my crutches, I was able to navigate the steps, slowly, but I could do it. I was always one to do it by myself, for myself, if at all possible. Generally, I didn't welcome help. Besides, if someone helped, and didn't know what they were doing, it did more harm than good. I fell down often, but could usually get back up on my own. Kindergarten went okay, though I remember being picked last for almost everything. The teachers, at the time, had not received special training on helping students with any type of physical challenge.

While in kindergarten we always had milk at our morning break. I was one of the few in the class that preferred white milk over chocolate. Johnny Haneys the local milkman would deliver the milk ice cold most often just before our break. We would often have some sort of treat along with our milk and different parents were responsible for bringing them. As I recall most of the time my treats were saltine crackers, which always went great with milk.

The first day of my first summer vacation after kindergarten— I am not going to say for sure this is from that day, but it is as I recall it. We lived in a basement house in Scotland. My mom made us poached egg on a slice of toast for breakfast. My brothers were out the door before me and were over playing in the grove of birch trees that was east of our house. I remember walking over there. By the time I got there they had taken off for parts unknown. I spent most of the rest of the morning sitting there playing in the dirt under the trees.

We eventually moved to a big house on the highway in Scotland. It was closer to Main Street and much closer to the elementary school.

When we lived by the highway, we were given a Daisy BB gun. At first, my brothers Mike and Jim managed to dominate its use. I didn't really get my chance until one day I was home alone with Mom. I'm pretty sure it was a weekday and, for some reason, the other boys were in school. I took the BB gun out on the porch and managed to get it loaded. I was randomly shooting at birds and stuff, while not hitting anything. But then, a car went by on the highway, and a window on the car ended up getting shot out. The guy went around the block, came back by, and came up to the porch. Of course, it was not possible for me to run and hide, so there I sat. He was not happy, and asked if my folks were home. I said Mom was in the house. I don't know what was said, but they managed to work it out. I told Mom I had been shooting at the sidewalk, and it must have ricocheted, which was not exactly true. I guess I was a better shot than I wanted to admit.

As a kid growing up in Scotland, stores were always pretty close to where you lived. My mom would practically have to threaten to beat my brothers to get them to run or bike to the grocery store (that was only two blocks from our house) to get a loaf of bread or something she needed for supper. I remember thinking, "How strange that they didn't want to, and that if I could, I would, in a heartbeat—any time, any place!" In fact, I would beg my mom to let me go and get what she needed, but she didn't know if I could. She finally relented and let me walk the two blocks to Gemar's Market. When I got the bread, the paper bag they put it in was small and barely held it. On the way home, I had to hold the bag and bread at same time to keep the bag from tearing, while, of course, also holding my crutches to walk. I had to stop about every 20 steps to shift and make sure I didn't drop my purchase. I was determined to get it home, all in one piece. I was successful, though the bag was a bit worse for wear from the trip.

One time we boys all got in trouble for something, no clue for what, but I guess it was serious. I think it was either a Saturday or a Sunday. After Mom left us, we decided we would get them, and run away from home! We packed pretty much nothing and headed to the one part of town we were forbidden to go to, down by the railroad tracks, where there were supposedly bums that would snatch kids and take them away. We decided we were going to ride the rails out of town! We spent a good part of the afternoon messing around down there, walking on this white stuff, that was some sort of residue from the trains, I remember that it was sort of soft and my crutches sunk in some and in some places sunk in a lot. After messing around for a while we got tired of it and headed home. When we got there Mom hadn't come home yet! So they hadn't even missed us! We did fess up to it though and as I recall later that day were went to Aunt Donna's for supper and heard that Janie and Kathy had done something similar that very day, though I seem to remember they had actually packed up suitcases to take.

My uncle Emil Orth, Donna's husband, died of cancer when I was pretty young. All I really remember was a lot of hushed talked, and doing some extra things like he got this new BBQ and grilled up this large sirloin steak marinated, and I remember what it tasted like to this day. Then all of a sudden he was gone. We kids didn't attend the funeral, I just remember my folks were really sad and that my dad brought home Emil's fireman's shirt. I remember he would wear it sometimes. I never asked if it was that he just happened to grab it, or if there was some special meaning to when he wore it, and I always kind of wondered about it.

Uncle Emil was also into photography. He had an 8MM silent movie camera and would often take movies of events like birthdays and Christmas. Years later when they were cleaning out at Grandma Sternhagen's they came across his equipment and, since I was into photography, they gave it to me. I had some fun times with that old camera and light rack and projector. I had it a few years before VHS cameras became the norm, and I made a few movies with my sister Beth and nieces and nephews. It was kind of fun: you could make people disappear or appear like magic; it had a single frame mode that allowed for a lot of flexibility; we even made a couple of stop action movies with my sister's little people playsets, and also with her Barbies. Many years later I had the honor of being able to convert the movies Emil made, that Jane had later had moved to VHS, to DVD and digital format, so now they can live on. During that time I find a very short clip of me walking without my crutches. I vaguely remembering doing that. I remember my dad was so proud that I could walk that way that he got ahold of Emil and they made the clip right away. I didn't walk very well and I never walked much that way, but I guess it meant a lot in a way.

One summer, they started little league baseball. I remember the first day of peewees. I tagged along with my brothers to sign up. Even though they were much more excited than I was, I was going along. The thing I remember most was the coach telling me, "Sorry, but there's no place for you on the team." It was one of those times I felt very crippled, even though I hadn't really wanted to get on the team all that badly. To be told you cannot really brings things like that home. It is probably why I have little or no interest in sports to this day. At the time, I could barely hit a grounder and could not hit an air ball at all. Years later, at CCHS, I did play a little baseball, though not organized or anything. It turned out, if I used a short bat and only hit with one hand, I could hit almost anything. I am just now realizing, that as a kid, I had tried to hit while standing, without my crutches and using both hands on the bat. This stance left me very unstable, and because my left shoulder is quite weak, it was impossible for me to hit. Whereas, when I hit one-handed, I was balanced, and the bat was more like my crutch, an extension of my arm.

My dad wasn't really much for most holidays, though there were a few Christmases when we got HO type race cars. He really got into that, and eventually mounted the track on a sheet of plywood to keep it together better for us. Later, when they would come to Sioux Falls to drop me off or pick me up at CCHS, we always went to the hobby shops to get cars and parts.

The one holiday I remember my dad really liking was the fourth of July. We always got a lot of fireworks and he seemed to really enjoy figuring out what to get and setting them off. Dad was almost as giddy as we were when the flyers would come out. The first day you could legally buy fireworks in South Dakota, we boys would go down to the local stand on the edge of town. We'd be waiting when they opened up, and would spend pretty much every penny we had, or could beg from my folks, on fireworks, mostly firecrackers. At that time, you could get a fairly decent pack for a nickel. It was also something where having crutches was an advantage. My dad, being a plumber, always had pipes around and the rule was we could only shoot our firecrackers from pipes. My aluminum crutches are basically pipes put together to make a crutch. Since I was still growing, they were adjustable. If you held in both buttons on the sides, you could make them taller or shorter. They could also be taken apart, which is what I did to shoot firecrackers out of them! The only real problem was that my brothers knew that as well, and often it was a bit of a problem getting them back once they'd been borrowed for shooting firecrackers.

One fourth of July we went to Susan Hirsch's family fireworks display. We often did things with the Hirsches, picnics and such. They normally had a fairly decent fireworks display. The one year I remember the Hirsch boys, Vic, or VJ, Fred and Tommy had setup a cool display with roman candles and rockets already planted in the ground ready to go. As they were lighting them, one didn't seem to work right, Fred was investigating and as it was dark was down pretty close to the rocket when it went off! It hit him just above the eye. As he was running around screaming we all thought it had taken his eye out! But luckily it had not. For many years I thought it was Tommy this happened to, but in July of 2015 when I mentioned this on Facebook Fred Hirsch, who I was friends with, came back and said it was him! I feel lucky that I had that story corrected because almost a month to the day later he had a massive heart attack and died within a day or two. In part that is what triggered my decision to just publish the first edition of *Normal for Me*: ready or not, better an imperfect book that existed than a perfect one that never did.

At one point, my Uncle Dick owned the laundromat in Scotland. He lived in Sioux City, so my dad managed it, did the maintenance, and took care of the washers, dryers, and the system. Once we all went with dad and he had gotten a bottle of pop for each of my brothers, but not me. He was teasing me that I wasn't going to get one. I cracked him in the shin with my crutch. Apparently, I got lucky. He was mostly shocked and just laughed. I got my orange crush! After that, when someone was teasing or giving me a hard time, Dad would say, "Just crack him in the shins."

Swimming was good therapy for me and the doctors recommended that I learn early. My parents enlisted a neighbor girl, Susan Hirsch, to help me learn to swim. She did so during the summers before the pool opened and in between the afternoon and evening sessions, when they would close it over the supper hour. It was one place I almost felt like the other kids. I could swim quite well and learned to float on my back and front. I wasn't fast, but I could float all day and I am sure I still could. Later, when I was the right age for swimming lessons, I remember going to them and the instructors apparently did not know I knew how to swim. In fact, they were quite worried I would be a problem and drown on them or something. When they told us, at the first lesson, to dunk our heads under, I did, of course. Since I could hold my breath, I didn't come up right away, and one of them grabbed me and pulled me up. I was like "Huh? Were we not supposed to hold our breath?" Later at, the end of the class, there was a test to see who passed. We needed to swim in the deep end to the diving board and back from the side. They left me until last, and then one of the instructors jumped in and swam beside me. I remember thinking at the time how foolish they were. I knew how to swim without touching bottom. I did that all the time. Of course I passed! Years later, before I was moving from Vermillion to Madison, I was at the laundromat in Vermillion. I was washing my clothes before the move, and Susan Hirsch was there! She was just moving to Vermillion, to take up some grad classes or something. We talked a bit, but sadly, we were just two ships crossing in the night.

The pool was only a couple blocks from our house and, during the summer, most of the kids in Scotland practically lived there, including us. We would be there when it opened until it closed, every day the weather permitted. My brothers would usually give me a ride on their bikes and I would leave my crutches and braces at home. Often, we would stop on the way home at Ed Pillars. He had horses in a fenced-in area by his house, right across from the pool. One time this proved a problem, as my brothers dropped me off there and took off for parts unknown. After quite some time, I figured they weren't coming back, so I ended up crawling home. It was about a block and a half, so it took quite a while. The most difficult part was crossing the highway, it took me a couple tries and I actually ended up having to roll down the other side to get out of the way of an oncoming car. I must have been quite a sight, but I made it and never said a word about it.

Ed Pillar was an interesting person in Scotland, a used car salesman and horse trader of the highest order. He was definitely a wheeler dealer. He was always very nice to me, and at one point he had traded for a pair of Shetland Ponies perfectly matched to pull a cart he had. When he got them home, he found that one had died in the horse van on the way. He decided to give me the other one. He named him Lucky, since he had survived, and I thought I was very lucky to have him. We kept him staked out around our house in Scotland, moving him daily to give him grass to feed on. Unfortunately I didn't get to ride him much: we didn't have a saddle, and Ed was looking for one but didn't find a suitable one, so my brother Mike was the one who got to ride him the most. He was quite gentle and I did have a good time helping take care of him. When winter came it was decided that he needed to go to my Uncle Paul Bickett's farm, Paul and his family had moved to a farm south of Scotland along Highway 46. There was a country school at the end of their driveway and unfortunately some of the boys there took great fun in teasing Lucky, throwing rocks to get him to run and buck. He ended up getting a bit wild and bit my cousin Vickie, so Ed had to trade him off. He ended up getting me a Toy Terrier named Eddie as a replacement. Eddie was very cute and knew a few tricks. He now along with Sandy followed us pretty much everywhere. He ended up getting hit by a car though while following my brother John on a fishing excursion a few years later. John brought him back and I went outside to have him die in my arms.

Chapter 3

I distinctly remember my first day of first grade. It was in the old grade school building, on the ground floor. Over the noon hour we all went outside, and kids were running up to the windows of our classroom looking in. I thought that looked like fun, so I was going to do it also. The only problem was that there was a grate over the basement windows directly under that room, and my crutches slipped through. I went down hard! I hit my head on the hard steel grates.

My Aunt Donna, as I always think of her

The fall produced a couple of nasty cuts, so, again I made a trip to see Aunt Donna so she could patch me up. I didn't go back to school that afternoon. When Mom got me home, she let me go outside and, of course, Sandy was right there. Mom had given me a piece of hard candy, and this is the first time I recall sharing candy with Sandy. He begged, as dogs do, so I took it out of my mouth and gave it to him. He kind of sucked on it a while, then I opened his mouth and took it back and sucked on it a while. We went back and forth until it was gone. We did it other times too, but that incident, because it was associated with that fall, sticks out in my mind. I was the only one other than my dad that could have gotten away with this. Others would have likely pulled back a bloody stump.

Other than that, first grade went pretty well, Dick and Jane and all. My favorite time was after lunch when the teacher would read to us. I remember her reading *Little House on the Prairie* by Laura Ingalls Wilder, among others. I also remember my mom would pack us a lunch and my brothers would normally come to my classroom where we would share it. My mom kind of went all out, as we always had a thermos of milk, along with one of soup, and occasionally even hot dogs. I would usually walk to and from school, which was about four blocks. If the weather was bad, my Grandpa Sternhagen would give me a ride. The walking was okay, other than the fact I couldn't really carry my books very easily. This wasn't too big of a deal in first grade, but became a problem later on. My brothers rode bikes and sometimes would give me rides, as well. Of course, I couldn't ride, though not for lack of trying, but no way. Normally, Jim would give me a ride on his bike, as he had a rack on the back. It wasn't a seat or anything, just a rack. He would also often carry my crutches laying them across the handle bars.

When I was in second grade, the teacher was an older woman. I will not call her a lady. She didn't really appreciate having me in her class and made no secret of that fact. My desk was right by the door and I could often hear her out talking with other teachers about her plight. As luck would have it, there was a student teacher assigned to our class and the teacher managed to pass along her negative feelings towards me to this student teacher. This student teacher went on to be hired to teach third grade the following year. This led to many problems for me that eventually ended up with me going to Crippled Children's Hospital and School (CCHS) in Sioux Falls, SD. Other than the teachers not liking me, I did fine in second grade.

In third grade, things got very difficult for me. First off, the classroom was on the second floor of the school and I had to walk up the stairs to get there. As I mentioned previously, the student teacher from second grade was now teaching third grade. It was impossible for me to carry my books and I disliked asking for help, so I started falling behind since I couldn't get my homework done in time. This led to staying in at recess most days. That part was okay, since, because of the stairs obstacle, I could barely make it down and back up again in the time allotted for recess anyway. I do remember looking out the window and watching the other kids having fun outside. I was missing out because I couldn't carry my books and I wouldn't ask for help.

There was a rule that you could not pass on the stairs. One side was for up and the opposite for down. Each day I made the effort to be on my way up long before the bell, so I would not be in anyone's way. One time, though, I was late getting started and there was a whole line of kids behind me, complaining about how slow I was going. When I came to the landing, a kid cut in front and started going up the stairs. I managed to grab the back of his shirt and threw him back against the wall. Well, he went running up the stairs to tattle, and luckily for me, my teacher was not yet in her room, but the fourth grade teacher, Mrs. Neumister, was. She had been a family friend for as long as I could remember. She came just as I was getting up the last steps and asked what happened. The kid had said I threw him against the wall. I said, "He was passing on the steps, and there is no passing on the steps." She asked the other kid if that was true, and he admitted it was. She had us both sit in our classroom until our teacher got back. I could hear her telling my teacher about it and could also hear my teacher defending the other kid and placing the complete blame on me. Since it was her class, she did as she wanted. I was disciplined and he was not.

During this time, my dad started managing a gas station in town that was right across from the high school. My brothers and I would spend a fair amount of time there. My older brothers would often pump gas, wash windows or check oil. We would all help sell the candy, pop, and ice-cream. In fact we would head there right after school. The elementary school got out 15 minutes before the high school, and even I could normally make it the two blocks to the station by the time the high school classes were released. The place was crazy busy then! The junior high and high school kids would all rush in before they needed to board the buses to go home. We would fill our pockets with change and stand there selling the snacks and making change out of our pockets. It was a good way to practice our money counting skills.

One time, coming home from the gas station, my younger brother, John, was walking right behind, trying to get me to hurry up. He was kicking me in the butt, telling me to hurry up. I kept telling him to knock it off. He didn't listen and that made me mad, so I swung my crutch around. It is probably good that a tree was in the way, because I broke my crutch on it, which is not easy to do. I am sure John would have been seeing stars if it had connected with him. Instead of laughing, he helped me return to the gas station to repair my crutch.

With my difficulty completing my assignments, they were often turned in just partially completed, and I guess that made it seem like I also had mental shortcomings. The teacher started treating me as if I was mentally disabled, as well. It became rather obvious. I remember the time I got to really surprise her though. We were all required to memorize a four-line poem and then recite it in front of the class. Since my last name starts with an "S" I was one of the last students to be called. Every student that had gone before me had needed prompting to finish. When it was my turn, I got up, made my way to the front of the class, and recited my poem perfectly! No prompting, no missed words! I then headed back to my desk. The teacher was dumbfounded, and asked me if I could do it again. I guess she was wondering if I had used some trick. I stopped where I was and once again recited it perfectly. I knew too, that even though I often didn't get my math homework done, I was quite good at math. That spring, it was decided it was in my best interest to go to a special school. Starting in April 1965, I was taken to Crippled Children's Hospital and School (CCHS) in Sioux Falls. Their school calendar differed from Scotland. While I was gearing up for summer vacation, they still had two and a half months to go. I felt it was a bit of a rip-off. At CCHS, we didn't get out for the summer until August, and then it was barely for a month, rather than the three in public schools.

Chapter 4

My mom was Catholic and my dad Presbyterian. He rarely attended church, and since it was a bit hard for my mom to manage on her own, I seldom went, and so I got to spend the time with dad on Sunday mornings. I remember him letting me sit on his lap and drive the pickup. We would often go to his plumping shop and have donuts by the little wood stove.

I was baptized Catholic and started attending church more often, as I went to catechism. When I was in second grade, it was time to make my first communion. My great aunt Mable Sternhagen was the teacher. Now you would think that being related and all she would understand, but I guess she was more like my regular second grade teacher and far from a caring aunt. She had it in her mind that I couldn't use my crutches as "it wouldn't look right." I could kind of walk without them, as long as I had something to grab onto like the pews as we went by, but when we got up to the altar area there were a couple steps and no railing. That was impossible for me without my crutches to help. She was adamant about it and my dad really stuck up for me. He wasn't one to say much or argue with people in public, but I remember him telling her and the priest that I was damn well going to receive my first communion with the rest of the kids and that I was going to use my crutches! They ended up with a compromise. I walked up the aisle without them, and my folks sat on the right side in the front pew and handed me one crutch so I could get up the steps. I have to say I was proud of my dad, but the whole thing left me with a bad feeling about church that lasted for some time.

In the fall of third grade, my Uncle Tom Bickett married my aunt Rose. Tom is my godfather, and had asked me be his ring bearer. My Grandma Bickett kept telling me I was going to have to wear a "Monkey Suit," which I thought was pretty cool. Imagine my surprise when it turned out to be a tuxedo!

Tom came and picked me up from school on Thursday, as I recall, and took me to my Grandpa and Grandma Bickett's farm by Winfred, SD. Friday he let me ride on the tractor with him while he plowed in the cable to run electricity to the mobile home he had moved onto the farm place. That night we went to the rehearsal in Madison, SD. It was raining, and we were running late. I remember hanging on for dear life as my Uncle Tom drove his 1963 Chevy about 90 miles per hour all the way there on very wet gravel roads. The wedding was the next day and I was determined to walk down the aisle without using my crutches. I managed that, while even holding the ring pillow, and once again, was handed my crutches when I got up to the altar. I believe it was by Grandma and Grandpa Bickett who were in the front row and handed them off to me.

Tom and Rose Bickett's wedding with me in my monkey suit. It is one of the few pictures of me standing without my crutches. Note that I could not stand with my feet together; I had to take this stance to be able to stand without my crutches.

Chapter 5

When I started school at CCHS, it was just after the Easter break. I did have a bit of a rough time adjusting, as it was a boarding school. There were many times that I'd had extended stays for surgery, not to mention when I first got polio and spent over a year in Omaha; but this was still different and it did take some time to get used to. At least I was always able to get my homework done without all the worries of having to carry books. I really didn't like being there and, in many ways, having to go there made me feel more handicapped than I ever had. At the same time, it made me feel like I at least sort of fit in. That was a feeling I really didn't have otherwise. Even at home, I always felt like I was an outsider looking in, or just visiting. I suppose that has a lot to do with the fact that I spent a good part of my formative years in the hospital, in particular when I went in at 18 months and didn't really come out again for a year. At that young age a person builds family bonds and I guess in a way my family bonds were more institutional than most. I eventually became much closer to many of my friends at CCHS than my own siblings. But even there, I was a bit of a loner and very independent. I've always followed the beat of my own drum.

One positive thing about attending CCHS was that there were always other kids around in similar or worse situations than what I dealt with. In fact, whenever you started feeling the whole "why me" thing, you saw others worse off than yourself who were handling it better. I have to say that was one of the most significant positive aspects of having to go there. To be very honest, if I had I stayed in the Scotland public school, I really don't think it would have ended well. Between the lack of facilities, the lack of specialized training of the teachers and staff, and the negative attitude displayed by some, I know I would have rebelled along the way and it would not have been good. Kids were already picking on me, even though I had my brothers to defend me. I carried a couple of 'aluminum bats'

with me wherever I went and I knew how to use them, but that
would have added to the problem in the long run.

*From the east side aerial view of Crippled Children's
Hospital and School now as it was when I attended.
The wing on the right closest is the classroom wing,
under in the basement is laundry etc. The further back
on the right was the boy's dorm area. Each dorm room
had space for nine beds, but often had up to 14, using
bunk beds. There was a bathroom connecting two
dorm rooms on each side of the hall. The further away
wing on the left was the girls' dorm on top with four
groups of 2, 4 bed rooms with bathroom between each
two sets. Below is the gym. The closest left side wing is
therapy on the top and the pool beneath. The old front
lobby and entrance are in the middle, a bit south of
where they are now.*

One area where I could always keep up with my brothers was
eating, and my mom was an excellent cook! This had some
side effects, as there was little I could do to burn those calories
the way they could, and it turned into excess weight for me.
This got worse during my first few months at CCHS. My mom
would send treats with me and then send care packages, too,

because I was young and away from home and she felt I needed comfort. I ate a lot of those goodies and loved every one. It didn't take long before they put me on a diet which, I guess, was both good and bad. I am not sure how much it helped. At that time, no one really addressed the underlying reasons for my overeating. To this day I have to watch my weight.

Dining Room at CCHS, sometimes during tours called "The Circus Room"; we never called it that though.

Meals at CCHS were very structured and predictable. I remember Monday breakfast was always pancakes, Tuesday, oatmeal, Wednesday and Thursday cold cereal, Fridays French toast. I don't remember most of the rest, except Tuesday night was roast beef. By the way, they did an excellent job of it. Another food memory was one Friday before lunch I smelled one of my favorites from home, deep fried shrimp. I thought, "Wow, what a treat today." Imagine my surprise when it turned out we were getting 'not such a treat' tuna casserole. I found out the shrimp was for the board of directors that were meeting over noon hour. I did not think that was fair at all! Often, after that, I would think of the board as the shrimp eaters.

School at CCHS was very different. The classes were much smaller and the teachers seemed to care more and work more with each child. The first couple years weren't all that eventful. I do remember my first fall when they were having a wheelchair football game between the students, The Gladiators, and the staff. One of the older kids asked me who I was for. I had no idea who the Gladiators were, but knew the staff, so I said, "Staff." Wrong answer! I got read the riot act and never made that mistake again.

One of the cool things at CCHS was an indoor, year-round, heated therapy swimming pool. This pool was great and I spent as much time there as I could. They also had PE. In my first week there, we were playing bingo. I had played bingo before, but this was different. They had this really cool basket that they would spin and then take out the balls that had the number on them. During our break, when the teacher went for coffee, being the inquisitive kid that I was, I wanted to give that thing a try, which I did. Unfortunately they hadn't latched it and when I gave it a spin the balls with the numbers went flying all over the place! Of course this was right when the teacher was walking back into the room! He was really very upset, yelled at me, and made me pick them all up. When I got them all back on the card, there were three missing. He made me look for them until the end of the period. Then I had to come back and look for them after school and during every gym period we had and after school most days, the rest of the year. Luckily for me, he was done at the end of that summer, so I only had to do it for three months. His replacement was Don Johnson, who was fresh out of college and from Olivet, SD, which is about 8 miles from my home town of Scotland. Things went much better after that. In fact, I got a ride home with him for Thanksgiving and a few other times along the way.

When I came home for the first summer or August vacation after I started at CCHS, things had changed radically at home. The house we had lived it was a rental and it had gotten sold almost out from under our family. My parents had decided to buy a house instead, but that takes time. Mike and Jim went up to my Grandma Bickett and John stayed with Grandma Sternhagen. My folks actually lived in the basement of the DX gas station my dad ran. The day I got home was actually moving day! They had found a house! It was right across the street from the Catholic Church; in fact, it had been the parsonage house before the new church was built and it had moved across the street to where it was now. I remember that day very well. Another change was that a Dairy Queen, later rename Dairy Inn as I recall, had opened in a new building kitty corner from my dad's gas station. My mom had John and I go there for supper that night. We had fish sticks and French fries.

Our new house in Scotland across from
St. George's Catholic Church

We slept that night on mattresses on the floor, in what would be our new house in our new bedroom, the south west corner in the upstairs, as it turned out, the hottest room in the house. I learned the hard way there is a right way and a wrong way to close blinds, when the sun was glaring in my eyes the next morning. We went downstairs. No one was around. There was a toaster and bread and butter on the table in the kitchen and that was pretty much all there was so far. Which was fine with John and I. I recall we were just finishing breakfast when the commotion started. Mike and Jim were back, with a fair number of my mom's family the Bicketts to get the move going. The rest of the move and the rest of the vacation were a bit of a blur. All too soon I had to go back to Crippled Children's.

Chapter 6

Fourth Grade at CCHS was much better, though I still hated the fact that I had to go there instead of being at home. PE went from much-hated drudgery to an anticipated class. On my first day back, I went down to the gym to start my search for the non-existent bingo balls. Mr. Johnson asked what I was doing. I explained my story of my inquisitive nature turning into a grueling task. He said that he actually had a note from the previous teacher suggesting that I needed to keep looking for them, but Mr. Johnson said we could just forget it. That certainly made for a step towards thing starting off on a better foot. He also increased our open swimming times. One thing I could never get enough of was swimming. The pool at CCHS was heated to a therapeutic warm bath temperature. I could occasionally take naps floating on my back.

Mr. Johnson in the warm heated pool at CCHS

My favorite class even then had to be industrial arts. With Mr. McCoy I became a special case to him right away. At the time of the whole bingo marble fiasco, he tried to help me figure out a way to make new ones to replace the three that I had been searching for. While the gym teacher was kind of mean and a bit ridiculous about finding them (as quite obviously they had been missing before I ever messed with the basket), Mr. McCoy took me under his wing and was one of my strongest supporters and my mentor from that time on. Along the way, he taught me additional things that few others had an interest in. These included both gas and electric welding, photography, and development of black and white film. He was also responsible for my interest in electronics. He helped me tinker with the old radios that were often donated to the school. We even managed to get a very old radio with big open fin air dielectric tuning capacitors to work!

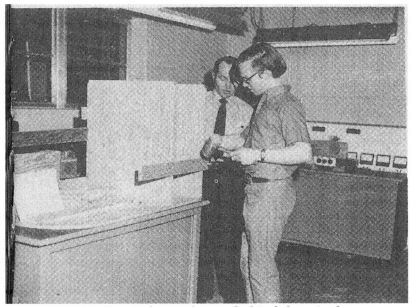

Mr. McCoy Industrial Arts, behind them is the electronics area where I spent a lot of my time.

School at CCHS was year round. There were a few long breaks of three or four weeks during the year. One was at Christmas, one over Easter and the final at the end of the school year in August. The new school year started over again in September. During the breaks, I would spend most of the time at home, but also would spend about a week at my Grandma and Grandpa Bickett's farm near Winfred, SD. I always enjoyed my time there. Uncle Tom and his family had a trailer house on the same farm, so I would stay at Grandma's house, and ate most of my meals there (my grandma was an excellent cook too!), but I would also spend a lot of time with Uncle Tom and his family. Tom worked the farm with Grandpa. They had a small dairy, and I got to help with feeding the calves and putting the feed out for the cows when they would come in. Tom would let me help with things. He was less protective than my folks.

Grandma & Grandpa Bickett home near Winfred, SD

Understandably, they were always concerned for my safety and wellbeing. Tom and Grandpa also had always been around me, so they were able to be helpful if I fell, which I did often. I remember once falling on the ice covered by water around the entrance to the trailer house. I was soaked and couldn't move at all. Tom just pulled me up and helped me make it into the house. He acted like it was no big deal. He was always good at making me feel less handicapped.

When I was little, I spent a fair amount of time at my Sternhagen grandparents, since they also lived in Scotland. My Aunt Donna, Uncle Emil, and their three girls, Janie, Kathy, and Nancy lived in Scotland, too. Janie was the oldest of the cousins on that side of the family, a year older than Mike. Kathy was the same age as Jim. Nancy was a few years younger than all of us. We would often go to Grandma's on Friday evenings or Sundays for dinner. I remember Grandma kept a meticulous house and all of us boys kind of intruded upon that. Especially me, as she had hard wood floors that do not mix well with braces and crutches. She had all these area rugs that also didn't mix well with my braces and crutches. The rugs were not rubber backed and one crutch on the edge and I was very quickly on my way to a hard meeting with the floor. She would often make me sit on one of those rugs while we kids played games. All the while, she watched me like a hawk. I am sure she was just concerned with my braces scratching the floors, but to a little kid, it seemed a bit much. More than once, after she had warned me a couple times and I was to the point of tears, my Grandpa Sternhagen would say, "Boys, lets go down in the basement." He knew how badly I felt and this was his way of rescuing me from more reprimands. My Grandpa Sternhagen was a cabinet maker and his workshop was in the basement. He was probably one of the nicest men I have ever known. When he took us down there he had hammers for each of us and would open the nail drawers and give us scraps of lumber and we would "build" things with his help. A few times, after dealing with the sitting on the rug thing, I would be mostly interested in just pounding very hard on nails.

My dad worked for Surge for several years. Surge is a company that installed and maintained milking systems for dairies. He would be gone all day most days and sometimes for days in a row. My Grandpa Sternhagen would often give my mom and us rides when the weather was bad. Once in a while, during the summer, Grandpa would take us fishing. He had cane poles for each of us and we would go to Lake Henry, just east of town. I don't recall ever catching anything, but it was a lot of fun.

We also spent a lot of time at my Bickett grandparents. It was always a lot of fun on their farm. We had two aunts, Silly (Cecilia) and Leona who were only a little older than my brothers and me. For the longest time I thought Cecilia's name actually was Silly. She was always laughing so I thought it fit her rather well. While Grandma Bickett also liked a clean house, she wasn't a fanatic about it. You certainly did not want to cross her, but you knew her bark was much worse than her bite. And I never felt like she was mean to me in any way.

I remember Christmas at the Bicketts'. Uncle Harold Arens would play Santa and he always made such a fun production of it. I don't remember what we ever got but I know we always had a good time there. I remember one year during a winter weekend visit we slipped into the ditch while on our trip home. Dad walked to a farm and then I think Uncle Tom came with the tractor and pulled us all the way back to the farm.

My first official cooking lessons were from my Aunt Kathleen Bickett. I was up at Grandma and Grandpas during my Christmas break from CCHS. I was always on hand, sort of in the way and such, so Kathleen decided to teach me to cook, starting with pie. She made the crust, and helped me with the pudding for the pies. We made a chocolate and a banana cream. The pudding was from scratch. I remember stirring and stirring; you couldn't leave them alone for a second or it would ruin it. Kathleen is almost as good a cook as my mom. I do remember though perhaps the same time, when she took a roast out of the oven and dropped it on the floor! Grandma instead of yelling said, as Kathleen was in tears about it, "It is fine, the floor is clean, it will be fine, no one will even know the difference."

Another time I was up there, Kathleen was dating her later husband, Larry Anderson. Larry was an interesting person. One of the first times I saw him, he had to show me his webbed toes! Larry was also a twin with his brother Leone. Larry had a 22 revolver that he let me shoot. I didn't hit anything but it was a lot of fun. During that same time they took me to very good movie, "The Guns of Navarone." Gregory Peck has always been a favorite actor of mine since then. After the movie we had a frozen pizza from a bar, Larry went in and ordered it, then we drove around until it was ready. Then we ate it in the car. I sat in the middle with the pizza on my lap. It had to be about the worst pizza ever! But it was a lot of fun.

I remember one time when working on I think perhaps Silly's car during the winter in the old garage at Bickettsville, it was at night and we manage to blow a fuse in the garage and there were no replacements available. When Tom Bickett asked me if I had a penny, I said, "I guess." He said needed a penny fuse. He took the penny and put it behind the blown fuse and screwed it in and the power came back on! I always wondered if that "penny" fuse was still in the fuse box in the garage when Timothy Bickett later had the garage taken down. By the way, I do not recommend the use of a "penny" fuse.

Over Easter break when I was 11 I was staying at my Grandma Bickett's, when my Grandpa Sternhagen died from lung cancer. He had been sick and in pain for some time, so it wasn't like it was a big surprise. I was out helping with the morning milking, when Grandma called me into the house. My mom was on the phone and she told me what had happened. I was devastated and mostly inconsolable. I remember sitting on the back step just outside the backroom crying my eyes out. My Uncle Tom came out from milking and asked what was wrong. When I told him and said I was mad that Grandpa had died and left me, I remember what Tom said: "Isn't Grandpa in a better place? As nice a man as he was, he is surely in heaven. Don't you want him to not have all that pain he had during his cancer? Maybe you are being selfish in wanting him to stay on earth with you, even though he was in pain."

It made a very big difference to me. I understood what he meant and it made me feel a lot better. Grandma and Grandpa were taking me back home the next day. That night I was sleeping in the far northeast bedroom and I swear my Grandpa Sternhagen appeared to me, telling me, "Market (that was his pet name for me) it is going to be okay. I am in a better place." I never again would sleep in that room, nor enter it other than in the day time.

Chapter 7

Shortly after starting at CCHS, I joined the Cub Scouts. It was a real advantage to be there as Scotland always had trouble keeping scouts going, but at CCHS it was a fairly constant activity. I don't remember a lot about the Cub Scouts other than I thought the blue shirts were very cool and I wore mine every chance I got. I really enjoyed Boy Scouts when I was old enough to join. I ended up going all the way to Life Scout, but I purposely stayed back from the Eagle Scout award. Even though I was only a couple of merit badges away, I decided I didn't want to go through with the big deal that was made when a person made Eagle. At the time it was enough to know I could do it.

In Boy Scouts, we did a lot of things, from learning to tie knots to every other thing Scouts did. I remember when we wanted to get our canoeing merit badges. Henry, our scout leader at the time, made a deal with Augustana College, which was using the pool at CCHS for their canoeing classes, to let us borrow canoes to use. He also found another troop of scouts to help us with getting the merit badges. It was really a lot of fun. I even learned how to get in from the water by myself, (not easy when you have little use of your legs). I was also able to right the canoe in the water with two people, both of us handicapped. The best part though, was after the lessons we would swim and mess around. One of our fun games was where Henry, who was a very big guy, would give the canoe a big push, with it loaded down with three to five of us from the middle of the pool. On one occasion when he was doing that we all agreed, ahead of time without his knowledge, to jump out and see what happened. Well we all jumped out as soon as he let go and since the canoe didn't have the weight in it, it sailed right into the wall of the pool, knocking out a few pieces of tile. Man, was Henry mad at us! Henry, who was in Sioux Falls from New York studying to be a Baptist Minister, could swear like no one else I have ever known.

The Boy Scouts once took a hike to the Western Mall, which is pretty much a straight shot about two miles south from the school. The rule was you had to push or get there and back on your own. Those of us that could go easier and faster took off and though it is a tough hike in a wheelchair, as it is very much all up and down hills. The down part is not so bad, almost fun, but the going up part is brutal. We eventually got to the mall after a bit of a scare, making our way across the very busy 41st street! We hung out there with none of us having any money at all. After an hour the slower ones showed up and we headed back. On the way back they made us stay within sight of the scout leader and other staff that were staying with the slower hikers. Since this seemed to slow our progress, we would push to the top of a hill, then fly down and sit at the bottom until the leader and others topped the hill, then take off and do the same again. It took three times as long getting back and we were all pretty beat by the time we got back to school. That is a long haul when are having to push yourself in a wheelchair up and down hills.

There were a couple of times in scouts that we got to go to the State Boy Scout Camp at Lewis and Clark Lake near Yankton. This was a week that was a blast! There was always fun stuff to do: swimming, canoeing, some hiking, though that was kind of a tough challenge, as at the time most roads were not paved and they were very hilly. We did all the things other scouts did, sneaking up on others' tents at night trying to scare them or trying to sucker others into snipe hunts. The first time I went was one of my first years in Scouts. Bill Poolster was the Scout Master then, very much the outdoorsman down-to-earth type of guy. He instructed us on how to do things as basic and nature friendly as possible. The second time we went was with Henry, who knew nothing of any outdoors stuff. These two guys were very opposite types of people. Bill was always strict by the Scout handbook kind of methods and Henry was just the "have fun and see what happens" type. I have to say, I feel lucky that Henry was the leader for most of the time I was in Scouts. He was also the recreation director, just as Bill had been, as that was part of the duties of the recreation director's job, to be Scout Master. Henry helped me more along the way than I know Bill would have. I eventually was made senior scout leader. This meant I would do things like run the scout meetings when Henry was not around or able to for one reason or another.

I remember another time we went, with Henry, to the Newton Hills Boy Scout camp during the winter! That was really different, as you can imagine. There was a big cabin there, which we were supposed to have to ourselves, but there was a snafu and we ended up sharing it with a couple of other scout troops. They didn't have regular heat, just wood stoves and a couple of fireplaces, so it got pretty cold at night. We scheduled the whole fire watch procedure, meaning one or two of us needed to stay awake to make sure the fire continued burning. We were all pretty tired, but we managed to stay awake; the fires stayed lit and the place didn't burn down. It was just for a weekend and was a good time.

One memorable time in Boy Scouts was when the Battleship South Dakota memorial was dedicated. A few of us along with other scout units were part of the honor guard. This meant standing in the sun for what seemed like two days but was more like an hour in the hot sun holding American Flags. It was quite an honor, I remember whenever I pass by the memorial.

We often had interesting escapades with Henry, also during the winter. We went to Lake Alvin, south of Sioux Falls for the car races on the ice. Henry decided that was rather boring, so he took us out on the lake ice in the school station wagon filled with eight to ten handicapped kids! We had a blast! He would speed up, put the car into a slide, do donuts; you name it we did it. Looking back on this adventure, it was crazy to say the least. There was actually open water in one area! Even though many of us could swim, we would not have lasted long in those temperatures and with winter gear on!

Another time during the winter we went to the CCHS camping area on Lake Brandt by Chester, SD. This lake "camp" was actually in a pasture about two miles down a dirt road, which had no maintenance during the winter. We got down the road okay and managed to make it part way to the camp area before we got stuck. With the help of the car bumper jack and Henry pushing and one of us driving, Elvis Tail I believe, we got out and managed to get turned back around. The trip out didn't go quite so well either, as we got stuck soon after we had started back. We managed to get out again, but broke the jack (which came back to haunt us later, when the next summer we had a flat on the interstate and no jack). Trying to get back on the road from the pasture, which was uphill and curving, didn't go well at all and soon we got buried pretty bad! After we heard a ton of swearing by Henry, he finally decided to try and walk to get help. The nearest farm was about a mile. This was on a Sunday afternoon and the farmer was taking his well earned afternoon rest. He was happy to come and pull us out with his tractor. He actually pulled us all the way back to the highway. I remember Henry trying to give the guy some money for rescuing us but the farmer, of course, flatly refused. When we got back to school, we made a card to send him and the school sent a check along thanking him. He in turn thanked us for the card and sent the check back. There are some people that just like to do good deeds; most farmers around South Dakota would do the same.

I have a lot of good memories of camping at Lake Brandt. As I mentioned, it was in a pasture, with cows present! The cows were very docile and nothing to be afraid of, except of course, by someone who was from New York. We always laughed at Henry whenever the cows would come down by the lake to drink as he would get all nervous and worried. My first time camping there, I was a Tenderfoot in Boy Scouts. Elvis Tail and I being the newest had to make breakfast. We had to come up with the menu, which had to follow the nutrition guidelines. We decided on: breakfast sausages, Wheaties and bread. Well, it was pouring rain when we were trying to cook the sausages, we got soaked! I remember we had to keep pouring the water out of the frying pan that we were cooking in and we had to sit out in the rain eating our breakfast also, where the milk in the Wheaties was more rain water than milk. But we managed. And it was a good hardy breakfast that met the nutrition guidelines!

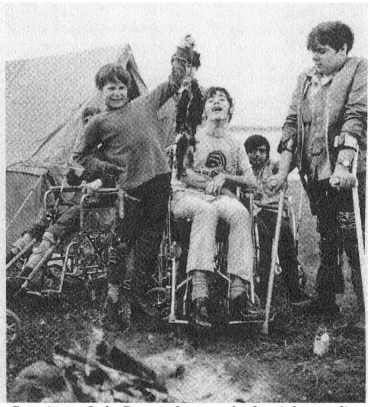

Camping at Lake Bryant. I am on the far right standing with my crutches, actually facing the camera, sort of.

At one of our camping adventures, Tony Paypay and I decided we would get up in the morning and go fishing in the fishing boat we had brought along. Henry said it was okay but we could NOT use the motor, just the oars. When we first went out all was fine, we rowed out and were fishing, but then the wind came up and we decided we better head back! Well, the wind had other plans and we ended up pushed into a little cove area that was quite a distance from the camp. Neither of us was able to walk out because we had both left crutches and braces back at camp. We kept trying to get the boat out of the cove and finally we decided we didn't really didn't have a choice but to try and start the motor. The boat's motor was one of those pull-cord types and we had a very hard time with it! Finally, Tony grabbed the cord and fell backwards off the back of the seat by the motor. He did this on purpose, to pull it hard enough and fast enough to start, which it did! I kept it going and together we managed to get us out of there and back to camp. Henry was a bit upset, but understood about how windy it had gotten. It all turned out well in the end as we both got our merit badges for rowing and motor boating.

A big storm came up during the night on one of our camping trips. Our tent was slightly downhill facing west, and managed to get swamped! We tried to keep the water out, but we gave up and went to the CCHS bus that was nearby. It was not very comfortable but at least it was dry. It was storming pretty hard and as we looked to the west/north west we saw three tornados! We kept watching, noting they were heading north east and we figured we were safe, so we kept watching, I am guessing they were about two miles away from us. During all this, Henry was in his tent with the kids who needed the most help, quadriplegics all on cots. The tent was in a different position and all high and dry and they were sleeping like babies. The assistant director from the school came frantically driving out there and came to us in the bus yelling there was a tornado warning and why weren't we in the ditch that was down the hill? We said we kind of figured out about the tornado warning as we had seen three of them a little earlier and the ditch as well as our tent was full of water. He got pretty hot and asked where Henry was and got hotter when we told him that he was fast asleep! He made us all get in the bus and head back to Sioux Falls, at 3AM, leaving everything out there! The next morning, a few of us went back with Henry to get things packed up and squared away. The assistant director tried to get us to implicate Henry in something to get him fired but we would not go there and did not cooperate.

When we first went camping the equipment we had was pretty well used. We had a few small pup tents that leaked pretty bad and some army mess kits that were in very sad shape. After Henry came things changed. He managed to get some donations to get some decent tents and other camping supplies. Eventually a nice pontoon boat that they had modified so that wheelchairs to fit through the doors was purchased from donations by a group from Yankton I believe. We had some great times camping and boating on the pontoon, Henry quickly got bored with fishing, so we spent a lot of time just boating on the lake. We would play man overboard with the lifejackets we were supposed to be wearing, tossing them over and then going around to recover them (without stopping of course). Henry even let us take turns driving the pontoon. A couple of brave souls—never me—would sometimes ride the pontoon out in front where the pontoons stick out from the deck and snag the lifejackets as we went by. Yes I know not very safe, but we never lost anyone, though we did lose a brand new lifejacket, that sank just as we were coming by. It turns out that jacket was apparently defective. When we got back to school, we tested them all in the swimming pool and I think we found at least one other than didn't float.

As I mentioned before we had some great times on the boat. One time, I am thinking in my senior year, we had a kid that was 19, and the legal age to purchase 3.2 beer at that time was 18. We were out on the boat with an orderly, who had come with us. Henry was back at the camp. We managed to convince the orderly to look the other way while the kid who was old enough to purchase, bought a 6-pack at the little bar on the other side of the lake. There were eight of us, so it really didn't amount to much but of course we thought it was great! It was in the evening and as we slowly continued boating around the lake, the motor quit! I happened to be the one driving and tried to start it. It started but quit again, then didn't want to start again at all. Eventually, the orderly and a kid (I am thinking it was Elvis, but not sure) decided to swim back to where our camp was and get the fishing boat we had docked there and tow us back. Well, they made it about half way to what we thought was camp and could hear people talking. It was the wrong camp, so they came back to the boat. The orderly, by this time, was very tired and couldn't get back in the boat. Luckily a couple kids (again not me) were weightlifters and managed to drag him back on board after a fashion. I kept messing with the motor and finally got it to start and headed towards where we now realized our camp probably was. It was the dark of night by now. We went a little further and it died again! I thought it seemed similar to when my dad's car had had a fuel pump go out, and though you can't really pump the throttle like you can a gas pedal, I did the best I could and got it started again and managed after starting and stopping to get it back to camp.

By now it was a couple hours or more after we were supposed to be back. Henry had driven the school bus to the bar on the other side of the lake, to see if anyone knew anything of our whereabouts and found out that a handicapped person had come in from a boat and bought a six-pack a few hours back. When Henry got back to camp and found us finally back, he was livid! He yelled at the orderly, then at us! He would not believe our explanation and we did not try to deny the purchase of the six-pack, but we stuck to the true story about the boat. In the morning, he went out in the boat and came back and he was even more upset because the motor worked fine! So he was convinced we were all lying. But what he had done before going out was get the other gas tank that was full, which had not been on the boat the night before, and he had hooked that up. This it turned out made all the difference! Later that day, when the gas level in that tank got down, the motor acted up again! What we did not know was that there was a little manual pressure pump thing we could have pumped and we could have gotten it to work. Since we didn't have any sort of flash light or lantern and it was dark when we had the problem, it would have been harder to figure out. In the end it turned out I was right; it was indeed the fuel pump.

Henry was a very interesting person; his one fault, we students thought anyway, was that he was fair about things. For example, every dorm, even the girls, got to go camping. That meant each dorm only got to go once a summer, with the exception of the Boy Scouts. We were always the first ones to camp in the summer. This was to ensure all the tents and equipment was in shape and good repair for the camping season. In case you were wondering, we actually did have to put up our own tents. The scouts also got to be the last at the end of the summer so that all the camping equipment would get a good cleaning and be packed away properly.

We used to go sledding on the hill that was at the time just outside the gym door, because that part of the building was cut into a hill. The part closest to the door is very steep then gets less steep the further away from the door you get. The middle was the best spot, as fairly steep and could get going, but not slam into the garage storage building that was just wide enough to get a service vehicle to the door. Crawling back up mostly without snow pants pulling a sled was a challenge, but hey, after you put on almost every pair of pants in your closet it wasn't to bad. I could last about an hour before I was almost frozen stiff. I remember never having decent gloves, and using socks instead. Normally we would just go out on our own. Initially the school had a couple of sleds that someone had donated, one large enough for two and the other a smaller one. Henry the recreation director at the time got a few of the, at that time, very new saucer type sleds. We had a blast when Henry would go out with us, as he would pull kids on the saucers and then sort of fling us down the hill past the part where the garage was in the way. I remember one time when Tony Paypay and I were out there late, both on the larger of the regular sleds, there was nice ice at the edge of the hill so we slid a ways onto the driveway, ending up in the middle of a large mud puddle, water all around us. The runners on those sleds are not designed to run very well on just wet pavement, and since neither of us had our braces on, there was no way to just stand up and take the sled out or anything, we ended up slowly pushing it with our hands in the wet puddle until we got to the frozen or dry area, then we had to crawl back to where our wheelchairs were. Seems like it took hours, though probably more like 20 minutes.

A couple times snowmobile clubs brought their sleds to CCHS, and actually let some of us drive them around by ourselves! It was a LOT of fun. CCHS hadn't taken up nearly as much of the block as it now does, so we could get going fairly decently, enough so I remember one Tony Paypay dumped his over. I am not really sure how he got it back up, but he did. We were able to make a good run from the yard that was then just north of the front door on the east side of the building, all the way around a full block west, then a full block south, then about one half block back east before coming back north again right by the ramp and swing sets, which of course were not being used during the winter. One of the orderlies had a group of friends that owned a few snowmobiles and he brought a couple of them around a few times as well. They were both Polaris brand, but a different one had a Wankel or rotary engine. I found that very interesting: it went faster and had more power than the other one, though other than the engine they were the same model. It also got much better gas mileage: it could run pretty much the whole time on much less than a thankful while the other would have to be filled up a couple times at least. As I recall it was a bit harder to start, but once it was running it was great.

Another fun activity was slot car racing. I had a 1965 Red Ford Mustang and I spent a lot of time figuring out how to make it run better and faster. I was fairly successful at it, as it was one of the fastest cars. It was different than the HO cars we had had at home when I was younger, but also they were easier to modify. A number of people donated track they had so we really had a very large set of tracks and could fill up a good part of the gym with it. We also did things like figure out what the speed of the cars was in relation to the size. It was a lot harder than without the use of computers or even calculators. If I recall correctly my Mustang do a quarter of a scale mile in about four seconds—pretty impressive I thought at the time.

2 lane bowling alley at CCHS doubled as a stage for Christmas plays, covered with Concrete blocks with plywood on top

There was a bowling alley at CCHS. They did not have full automatic pin setters. Someone had to put the pins manually in the setter, then pull the cord to have it set them. Actually it was kind of dangerous as if you were still in the pit when the ball came down and hit the pins you could easily get hurt, even sitting on the bench above a couple times came close. Hard to believe but we, as most "normal" kids would do, often would stay in the pit and then quickly try to get out of the way at the last minute. Looking back it is lucky no one ever got seriously injured. A few non-reported bumps and bruises here and there.

Chapter 8

I have to say I was often a bit of a handful at CCHS. It seems like I got in trouble fairly often and most often with Elvis. I am not sure why, but we must have thought a lot alike! Elvis was Native American from Porcupine, SD, on the Pine Ridge Reservation. He also had polio and was about a year older than me, yet we ended up in the same grade. One of his special talents was that he played guitar and sang, and used to make up some pretty nasty versions of current hits. He also was far more confident with the ladies. Polio mostly affected his legs, but the mirror image of mine, meaning his left was far better than his right and in my case it was the other way around. His arms were much better and more normal than mine. Elvis was a pretty good athlete, while I was just mediocre. He was the quarterback on our wheelchair football team and I the center. Wheelchair football is different in that the center faces the quarterback with his back to the other team, while the rest of the team faces the center and the other team. I did make a few critical touch downs though. Elvis and I had it worked out! You see the center can also block as soon as he snaps or throws the ball to the quarterback, but instead, I would just sit there, maybe block a little, but mostly just sit there. Then every once in a while, we would get in the position to need only a couple yards for a first in 10, or more than once we were right at the end zone and that is when Elvis would get closer than usual. I would hike him the ball and he would hand it back to me and give me a push back. More than once, the other team didn't even know what happened to the ball until I was in the end zone completing a touchdown.

As I mentioned above, I was never great at sports nor was I all that interested in them, but I did play on the CCHS Gladiators football and basketball teams. We would play against groups, and sometimes teams from Augustana College or Sioux Falls College, but only in the off season, as they didn't want their players getting hurt. The teams switched their specialty. In other words, we played football against their basketball players, and we played basketball against their football players. The rules for wheelchair sports are somewhat different. All players must be in wheelchairs and you could only use two of your extremities to propel yourself, for example I used both arms; Keith, who couldn't use his right arm, used his left arm and a leg. Of course, we generally had the advantage since we spent much more time and some of us all of our time in wheelchairs. Often the opposing team players would have great difficulty in the wheelchairs, everything from falling over, to forgetting and jumping up out of them to make a shot, which of course was a foul. Every year we played the CCHS staff, and generally the CCHS alumni in football for our homecoming game. We would most often play both in basketball as well.

CCHS homecoming actually became something for a few years there. We had parades in the gym with floats we had made. My class went all out one year, with a 4'x8' plywood place on a wagon, pulled by one of the few power wheelchairs there at the time. We even did the whole chicken wire with tissue paper flowers with a bunch of boxes taped together one on top of the other as a computer with a length of computer paper coming out of the top box that said something like "Gladiators will beat the Alumni."

The staff games were blood and guts, with the whole touch football thing kind of going out the door. I remember one year during a game, when I was the center, and had recently had surgery so my one leg was elevated, the ball was snapped and I hit one of the staff hard sideways. With my elevated leg, I kept pushing. He ended up first on one wheel, then completely tipped over. He barely crawled out before the chair collapsed on him. The alumni games were a bit different. We didn't feel the same blood lust, but they sure did! I think it was to maintain honor for them to beat the current team.

Every year we also did a couple of road games. This was in basketball, and more of an exhibition game and usually part of a fundraiser. One year we were undefeated. At a game in Iroquois, SD, the game was against a number of high school coaches from around the area. We had played them and beaten them soundly in past years, but this particular year, they decided to try and change that and for about a month before the game was scheduled, they rented a bunch of wheelchairs and practiced. This turned out to be a real game, and ended up going into triple overtime! We did finally win, but only by two points. When we played away games, CCHS would let us have one a year where we stayed overnight. One year we got to stay overnight in Huron, SD, and we did like most other high school kids at the time would have done: raised hell! This incident included locking a kid, clad only in his underwear, out of the motel room! But to make matters worse, it had an outside entrance, it was March and it was three o'clock in the morning! He created quite a ruckus as he was pounding on the door and yelling to get back in. We were lucky we didn't get kicked out. The motel was fully booked and our room was not near the staff's rooms, so they never actually found out. (At least as far as we knew they didn't, as we didn't get in trouble.)

Elvis and I got caught smoking twice in a row. The first time was just plain stupid and we were still grounded for breaking this rule. The second time we were down in the boy's room by the classrooms just after supper, having a smoke. We were in a 'quasi legal' area to be in as we really weren't supposed to be by the classrooms after supper, but the restrooms were sort of neutral territory and that is where we had our smoke. We heard someone coming so quickly flushed our smokes and were just going out when an orderly was coming in, and of course he asked if we thought it smelled like smoke in there. We told him the janitor had just been in there to empty the trash and he was smoking. In the 1960s, there were not designated smoking areas and the janitor, since he cleaned up anyway, pretty much smoked wherever he wanted. The orderly didn't really believe us, but what could he say? We told him we had to get back to our dorm as we were still grounded and it was time for us to be on top of our beds.

The dorm was laid out with four beds on the side with the door and five beds on the other side with an aisle running down the middle. Between each bed were the nightstands for those beds. This was where we would park our wheelchairs. Elvis and I had beds next to each other. The orderly came in a little while later and sat in my wheelchair that was between Elvis and my beds. He started laying a guilt trip on us, saying he really thought we were smoking in the boy's room and that what bothered him the most was our lying about it. He kept coming back and interrogating us but we held fast to our story that it was the janitor. He then said if we would just tell the truth he would not turn us in. He restated that we should tell the truth since it was worse to lie. Finally after a couple hours of that, Elvis and I were getting tired of it and looked at each other and decided to come clean. The orderly said, "Thank you for being honest," got up and left. Five minutes later, the nurse in charge came down to our room and was down yelling at us, putting us on report and telling us we would be further grounded. We were stunned! Talk about a liar! We chose not to speak to that orderly much after that.

What happened later bit even harder. If you got caught smoking or something like that, you had to go to one of the directors of the school. At one time it had been the director, Dr. Morrison, but he had recently delegated that to the assistant director but the assistant happened to be out of town. So we were sent to see Dr. Morrison after all. He told us he was not in charge of discipline anymore, but wanted to talk to us anyway. We told the complete story, the full truth of exactly what had happened and how we felt betrayed by the orderly and really thought that it was unfair. If we had stuck to

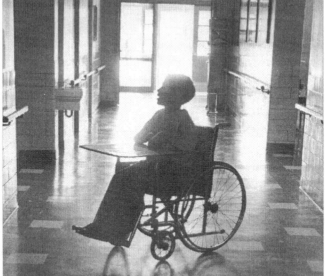

Unknown boy sitting in front of elevator in main hallway up front; behind him is Dr. Morrison's office, to the left is the classroom wing where the boy's

restroom we were smoking in is; to the right is the
therapy wing; straight ahead it the front door.

They could have never gotten us on our story (that the janitor was smoking) as there was absolutely no way to prove anything. Dr. Morrison agreed and said that when the Assistant Director got back in a couple days, he would talk to him and explain what happened and that he thought we should not be further punished. At that point, when we left his office we both decided and pledged to each other to quit smoking. We felt Dr. Morrison had been fair and had made some very good points and we did not smoke again.

When the assistant director got back, we were called into his office. He said Dr. Morrison had talked to him and explained everything, including that Dr. Morrison's opinion was that we should not be further punished. He said he did not agree and while he was in charge of discipline, things would be his way. First, we both had our grounding doubled, then I was told I had to write a letter to my folks telling them how I had broken the rules and been caught smoking. He told Elvis that since his parents were Indians, they probably could care less so he would not have to write a letter. I don't know which was more offensive, but we were both stunned and of course followed the adolescent, screw-you attitude. Before the day was out we had both started smoking again, though we were more careful and never got caught again. It was Friday and I had to hand the letter in on Monday, which I did, but it was not what he wanted. In the letter I stated I thought it was completely unfair and laid out exactly what had happened. The assistant director was very upset with me and said, "So this is the attitude you are going to take?" I said "Yup!" To be honest I don't know if he actually mailed it or not, but it did lead to my smoking habit for the next ten years or so. I am certain, knowing how I am, had he gone with Dr. Morrison's recommendations, I would have never smoked again. When I did finally quit, I only quit once and have never smoked since.

Chapter 10

While at CCHS, we always put on a fairly big Christmas program. The first year I had recently had surgery and was stuck being mostly in a bed, or in a wheelchair with elevated legs, so I was in the choir. There were usually three plays that were presented. They were presented by various grade levels: youngest or lower grade, one for middle school or middle age groups, and one presented by upper grades and high school. One year when I was in high school, I ended up playing Santa in the little kids' play, which was pretty cool as I got out of class for their practice times, plus I got out of class when the high school practiced as I would be the only one in class room. There was a drawback and that was that I had to be on the stage the whole time during the little kids' play, since the premise of that play was kids telling Santa what they wanted for Christmas. Another year I remember being the wind in "The Little Match Girl" and the little Match Girl was played by Penny, whom I had a bit of a crush on. Though I had to be on stage the whole time during this play, I didn't really mind all that much, because Penny had to be on stage the whole time as well.

The time between Thanksgiving and Christmas was always one of the best at CCHS. The school would be incredibly decorated, and always felt so festive. I particularly liked the medium sized individual twinkling lights that ran all around outside of the east facing side of the building. I used to sit in the front lobby for it seemed like hours, just looking out at them in the pine garland around the windows. They would always really decorate the place they had many large wood decorations, like sleds or snowmen that they would hang from the ceilings in the hallways, kind of like the way downtowns do, with "Merry Christmas" banners and the like. The doors of the classrooms they would wrap like presents with festive wrapping paper, ribbons and bows. As I recall they also had a large Santa's sleigh with reindeer they put on the roof of the building. Frankly, I think the school would almost have put the Griswolds to shame. Often different groups would come, caroling or putting on some sort of program. I have to be honest, I didn't care for them all that much, unless they were during class time when I could get out of school. Of course now looking back, I know that people really had their hearts in the right place, even if I didn't appreciate their talents.

The Elks club would always put on a big Christmas party for us. They would take us to their lodge, at that time in downtown Sioux Falls, I honestly don't know the exact location, since to get us all there in our wheelchairs, the would bring a big semi truck moving van, and with ramps load us all up in the back and then unload us at a loading dock when we got there then upstairs in a large freight elevator. A few weeks before, the ladies from the Elks would come around over noon one day and get a list from us of what we would like for Christmas in the under $5 range. The only one I remember is one year Mark Folk and I both asked for Catholic bibles. I learned they actually cost a bit more than the allotted $5 but they made an exception. I eventually lost the bible, but always keep the memory. The Elks party was on a Sunday afternoon. They would have a program with local talent, and lots of food, hamburgers and hotdogs, with Elk members walking around with bottles of ketchup and mustard—one of the few times that diets were pretty much ignored.

One year, at the Elks party, there was some buzz about someone special coming. We all thought it was just Santa for the littler kids, but turns out it was Andy Williams and Roger Miller! Now I did know who they were, though Andy Williams was much more my mother's style. Roger Miller had a number of songs that were just fun songs that crossed many music genres. After we got back to the school, again some buzz was going around, and it turned out we were all invited to go to their show at the Arena that night! So basically we got packed back up in the truck and hauled to the Arena, with almost front row seats, though the place was pretty packed. It made for a long, exciting day.

One year, the play was about putting on a Christmas play. It was quite interesting as some small plays were performed within the main play. In this play I was one of the three wise men, or "three wise guys" as we nicknamed them. What I remember the most about that one was that Tony Paypay sang "Silent Night" in Lakota. If you have ever heard this, it actually sounds pretty awesome! The irony to us was that even though Tony was a Native American, he was not Lakota. I believe he was Cheyenne. He did not speak either native language, but he learned the words phonetically.

Tony was another interesting friend at CCHS. If I wasn't getting in trouble with Elvis, I was probably getting in trouble with Tony. We both shared the common pastime of reading. I read mostly books and Tony enjoyed comic books. Tony was at CCHS because he was shot in the back with a .22 rifle by his little brother when he was nine years old and his brother was only four or five. Tony was out shooting at targets, and had set his rifle down to go reset the cans that he was shooting at. His little brother picked up the rifle and shot him. Interestingly enough, Tony ended up being very close to his little brother and he was later devastated when his brother drowned while swimming with some older boys near Mobridge, SD, where Tony was from. My only real fight I got into at CCHS was with Tony, and I ended up with a black eye, which I reported came from falling. I don't remember what caused the fight, but the black eye ended it and we remained friends.

Tony and I ended up sharing smaller apartments twice while we were at CCHS, due to overcrowding in the dorms. We could pretty much take care of ourselves and they had a rule that we were not supposed to lock the doors so that the staff could check on us whenever they wanted or should it be on occasion to see if we were still following CCHS rules. In reality, they pretty much left us alone. The first apartment was really nice. We also shared this apartment with Glen, who had spina bifida. This apartment had a living room with a hide a bed, which is where I slept, and a bedroom with two single beds, which is where Tony and Glen slept. Also, there was a small kitchen. We had no food to put in it, however I was always making ice in the freezer. This apartment was initially created for parents who would come with their younger children to learn how to better take care of them. The children would normally then go home with the parents who had been trained how to better take care of them. Later we were in a much smaller apartment, with just a bedroom and ½ bath. This is where they would house PT (physical therapy), OT (occupational therapy), or ST (speech therapy) students when they stayed for their internships. We always thought (or were told) one of the reasons they put me in the apartments was to split up Elvis and me.

Another time when I got in trouble, actually I am not sure for what, the school decided that I was being childish and they moved me down one dorm age level. This really kind of backfired on them. What happened is since I was the oldest in that dorm, I quickly became the leader of a sort of 'gang.' The boys in that dorm would do anything I said. I never asked, but they probably would have even fallen on a sword, so to speak and take the blame for me. It actually never came up, but that is the kind of following I had! They continued to follow me even after my interment with them was over. I think it was a month-long stay. I was often called upon to mediate disputes among them and to intervene on their behalf with the staff, particularly if they were having problems explaining their point of view.

Keith was another friend of mine. He was originally from Brookings and was there due to a problem with carbon monoxide in his family's home. It was a very sad story. His sister had died; his mother ended up with some serious brain damage issues and his dad, though mentally fine, had lost an arm because of the incident. Keith had lost most of the use of his right arm and some use of his right leg. He could walk reasonably well and he also had some speech problems. One of the things that I remember shows how we could push or challenge each other in our learning and dealing with disability. Keith had trouble buttoning his shirt. When he would get someone to help him and they would ask why he couldn't do it himself, he would say, "One hand." I actually taught myself to button my shirt with only my left hand, though I am very much right handed. When he said that to me, I said, "Oh really?" and I proceeded to button my shirt with only my left hand. After that he went to OT (occupational therapy) and made sure they taught him how to button, of course using 'one hand.' It was the kind of thing one disabled could do or say, when no one else really could. Keith and I became good friends and had many interesting adventures together.

We sometimes had slumber parties at CCHS, at least once a year. Generally during the winter months, we would have a sort of slumber party for our dorm room. There were normally between 8 and 12 students per dorm room. It would be held on a Friday night, mostly in the occupational therapy or OT area, because they had a kitchen there along with lots of cool things and games and such. We would try to stay up all night, often also going to the gym for part of the time for basketball games to try and stay awake. We would make homemade pizza, popcorn and other treats. This was back in the '60s, so TV was pretty much done by about midnight. One year someone had the album by Napoleon XIV (Pronounced spelled out X, I, V) and we played it pretty much non-stop. The album of course included his only real hit "They are coming to take me away, ha ha" but also many other fun songs.

A one point somehow they got a bunch of I think Shakley products, including an all purpose cleaner called Ziff. The cleaner wasn't important to us, but the squirt bottles they got along with it were. We found were they were stored, many cases of them, and we liberated a fair number of them, hiding them where we could, then the water war was on! Most of us carried four of them, two in our hands, or in the front of our wheelchairs some place, and then two more behind our backs in the wheelchairs where no one could see. We would eventually get caught and the staff would take away the first two, then as soon as they were out of sight we would pull out our backups and away we would go again. We managed to keep it up off and on for a couple weeks before they figured out where we were getting them from.

Somewhere along the way they got a couple of BB guns for us to practice with down in the gym. They were kept very restricted, but the BBs were not. We found that if you kept a few in your mouth, and had a straw handy, it was pretty easy to do the peashooter type thing with them. Not all that safe as it turned out, no eyes put out, but one girl managed to get one lodged in a cavity in her tooth and had to go to the dentist to get it removed.

A favored activity was not exactly on the schedule: raiding the kitchen. It would often be rather an elaborate affair, with a number of us involved, often from more that one dorm room. We used a series of lookouts, along with walkie-talkies. That is often where I came in: getting the walkie-talkies to work and work together.

The kitchen was downstairs and the main doors were unlocked. Most of the food was kept in locked pantries and coolers, except for ice-cream, which was kept in an older ice-cream freezer exactly like the one my dad had at his DX gas station in Scotland. And all of us that were normally part of the raids kept spoons hidden in our night stands.

We knew the schedule of pretty much everyone working in the evenings, where they were, where they would be and when. So with the lookouts in place a few kids would sneak down to the kitchen, and using a large stainless steel wash basin, would load it up with ice-cream! We would take only a few scoops from each of the containers and only from ones that had previously been opened, then sneak it up to often one of the younger kids' dorms where the lights were already out, and we would all dig in with our spoons. There were sometimes as many as ten in on the caper, so we each never really got all that much. It was more about the fun and excitement of getting away with something. We never got caught and really have no idea if they ever really suspected; we would only normally do it a couple times a month, though once in a while it would be a number of days in a row, until the heat was on, then we would lay low for a while.

Every once in a while on Friday nights we would order pizza. At the time the only place you could do that was from Chicken Delight, and even there as I recall we had to use a taxi cab to deliver it. Again this was a fairly elaborate affair, though with full knowledge of the staff. We would each chip in whatever we could, and someone would keep track of who chipped in what and that would dictate how much pizza each person got. Normally there would be a minimum amount to chip in. As I recall the pizza was always pepperoni, which was fine by me. It was some of the greasiest and honestly not very great pizza, but at the time it seemed the best in the whole world.

Another good friend that I remember well was Mark Folk. He along with some of his brothers had muscular dystrophy. During that era the prognoses for MD patients was not very good. Mark was probably the smartest person I ever knew. He was about a year older than me and we used to play games together quite often. We'd play Monopoly games that would last for days. There was also a board game called Conflict that was about war. We would modify the rules so that the games would last a long time. Another board game we enjoyed playing was Stratego. It was a little more common than the Conflict game. I think he liked the fact that I at least gave him somewhat of a challenge, although I know he took it easy on me and could have beaten me anytime he wanted, but then who would have been left? Years later my brother Mike who was a truck driver and was always trying to find ways to beat me at games came home with Stratego, saying now he had me in a game I could not beat him at. I just laughed and pounded him into the ground: after having held my own with someone like Mark Folk, this wasn't even a challenge.

Mark weighed about 80 pounds soaking wet. He was very skinny and physically slight in his wheelchair. Often times he would be the one to volunteer to get snacks when we went to events at the arena or other venues. He would get in line and bump the person ahead of him in the ankle with his wheelchair; they would turn around ready to yell at someone and there he would be with an innocent look on his face and they would say sorry and let him move up in line. He would often do that to good looking girls as well, and about one in ten ended up in his lap where he would be very apologetic. Of course we all knew what was going on, but none of us had the guts to try it. I sometimes felt Mark was a bit fatalistic, a bit of a short timer.

For a while Mark had a girlfriend named Mary, who was in his same grade and very cute. She had gotten something called a Harrington Rod, to straighten her spine, which meant she spent most of her time on a cart, which was like a gurney but had back wheelchair wheels in the front so you could lay on it and push yourself. I spent some time on carts as well due to a scoliosis from polio. Mark and Mary seemed great together and hit it off rather well. They would often be seen holding hands or doing homework together. That is until Howard showed up. He was an early artificial hip patient and had gotten a bad infection and they had to remove it and wait quite some time for the infection to heal and later replace it again. Howard was your classic bad boy. His family was in the carnival business so he had no real permanent home. They would travel all summer and wintered in different places. He was able to get Mary away from Mark, and Mark pretty much just gave up on her too quickly. I always thought it was kind of sad, but I also understood. Last time I saw Mary she had devolved into some sort of flower child.

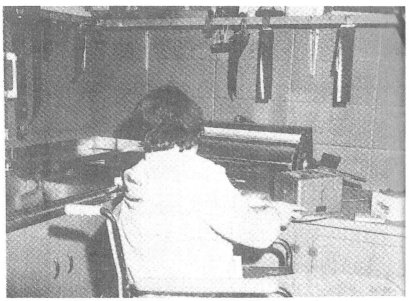

Me in the darkroom at CCHS. I was always more comfortable behind the camera rather than in front of it.

Probably my favorite present for Christmas or other times was film for my little Kodak instamatic camera. I would normally get mostly black and white film for a number of reasons. It was much cheaper so I could get more. It needed less light so I could take more pictures without using a flash, and most importantly I could develop the film myself in the darkroom that was located in the industrial arts area at the school.

The darkroom was sort of my sanctuary or fortress of solitude. I often spent many hours processing my film and photos. The staff would pretty leave alone since if you opened the door while developing whatever you were working on and hadn't yet been fixed, the process that completes the developing, would be ruined. I have to be honest I sometimes would just go in there and read the whole IA class period. But most of the time I spent trying to get the water bath the right temp, and processing film and photos. I learned a lot about exposure time and the distance between the enlarger and the paper, and how everything affects the final outcome. Once in a while other students would intrude on my domain, but most bored quickly and after a couple times never came back. One exception was Howard Mills. He was there because of a hip replacement gone bad and had spent some time working as a helper to a photographer in a carnival I think. While he did spend some time there and sometimes actually helped and developed film, he was mostly there to get out of doing industrial arts or other classes. We got along ok, but I never really got over him taking Mary away from Mark Folk. He would often talk about her and not in the kindest of terms.

One project that I did work on with Howard was trying to make a portrait of Mr. Anderson, the high school teacher. It was an anniversary of his working at CCHS, though I am not sure which one. We spent a fair amount of time getting him to pose without knowing what it was for. Howard had gotten hold of some cheap film that fit an old camera the school had, so we used that. Unfortunately, it was during the winter and we couldn't go outside. The only lighting we had was a set of lights from a seldom used movie camera the school had and they were nowhere near bright enough. Coupling that with the cheap film—which as it turned out was cheap because it was expired—we took a lot of pictures and processed a lot of film, but never ended up with an acceptable portrait.

When I was at CCHS, Captain 11, the local kids show host on KELO TV in Sioux Falls, would always come for his birthday party at the school. We would have cake and ice-cream and watch the John Wayne movie "McClintock." I am guessing it was his favorite. Due to my connection with Mr. McCoy I was also the A/V expert and often ran the movie projector for programs like the captain's party. One year, I am guessing I was about 14 at the time, the captain was into scuba diving and decided to give a demo on his birthday. Not sure how it came about but I was selected to participate with the captain. It was quite an honor. He gave me a lesson on how to breathe and how things worked. Then they brought in the rest of the kids and we did a demonstration! I also then ended up running the movie that day as well, my hair still wet from the diving.

While I was at CCHS they made a promotional movie about the school, and the things we did there. It was kind of an exciting time as we got out of class fairly often during the couple weeks of shooting, either to be part of some scene or because they were using some area and needed us out of there. I ended up in a couple minor scenes, but for me that wasn't the best part. The best part was that being the A/V kid, they would often send me to places to run the projector for some group or another. I even knew how to splice the film if need be. And of course the best part of all that was, if I was running the projector some place, I was also getting out of class.

Sherry Young came to CCHS for high school. She was from California but her family had roots in South Dakota. She was a year older than me but in the same grade and, like me, she was a polio survivor. She had gone to public school up to the time for high school, but the public high school in her home was not accessible, so she ended up at CCHS. Her arms were basically normal, but her legs didn't have a lot of movement.

In the beginning, we didn't actually get along all that well. I was and am a bit of a smartass and though she was somewhat attractive, she seemed to me to be a bit of the valley girl type so we kind of clashed. I remember one time when we were in psychology class, she was flipping through the book and came upon a picture of a crazy looking person. She pointed at it and said, "That is your dad." I knew who it was, so I said, "I wish": it happened to be Albert Einstein.

Eventually Sherry and I got along and after Dean Hansen came, they started dating and I was very close to both of them as we all graduated together. Dean had been in a car accident and because he was not wearing his seatbelt he ended up breaking his back. His arms were normal; in fact, he was a weightlifter at CCHS. He could bench over 200lbs. Although a paraplegic and had no use of his legs, nor much if any feeling from the waist down, he attained great strength in his upper body. Most polio survivors on the other hand have 100% sensation. I later lost contact with Sherry when she moved to Florida. Part of my point here is we were like a bunch of brothers and sisters at CCHS, which is both good and bad. Part of the bad was we rarely ended up dating, as it would be like dating your sister: yuck!

My Cousin, Leo Bickett, son of my Uncle Tom and Aunt Rose, who has spinal bifida, ended up at CCHS while I was still there. Leo is 10 years younger than me, so we weren't there very long together. I remember I used to sometimes go down to the little boys' dorm where he was and read bedtime stories to them; I occasionally would make up bedtime stories, often scary, and would use their names in the stories.

Chapter 11

Polio affects the motor neurons that control muscle movement. Excessive exercise, such as physical therapy, can further damage those remaining good motor neurons. At CCHS I did have some physical therapy, not to exercise to build muscles but rather to help me learn how to get by. For example, how to fall properly without getting hurt, how to climb stairs, how to walk outside and how to deal with other activities that could pose a challenge. Part of the helping me fall and get up properly instructions may have involved some 'tricks', such as being tripped by the physical therapists! Yes, they would actually try to trip us, not to hurt anyone, but to learn. First it would be by the padded floor mats in the physical therapy room. Later, as we were catching on, it would be walking down the hall, and when you fell, either from being tripped by them or just fell, as I often did, you had to get up by yourself. This was fine with me, as I had always wanted to do it by myself. I hated it when I was little and people would try to help me up, especially when they didn't know how to do it the correct way—their assistance usually caused far more harm than good.

When learning how to go up the stairs, there were times when I would be required to take the stairs whenever possible, rather than the elevator, even to the point where it made me late for class! I still had to use the stairs, sort of my prescription or PT rules. When going down the stairs with crutches the best way was to use one railing and one crutch. I was to hold the one crutch for the hand that was using the railing in the hand used to walk with the other crutch. This is a bit awkward and to be honest, I would often go downstairs by first tossing one crutch down the stairwell, so I didn't have to carry it. I know this does not sound safe and it is not, but to be truthful kind of fun. This often led to a staff member running in to the stairwell to see who had fallen, which was a bit of a devilish bonus to me. A risky dare taken on by some of the students, that I never did, was to try and go down the stairs in a wheelchair. This would have been tried on a dare or challenge. I was way too chicken for that. I do remember one time, when a boy named Larry jumped on the lap of a kid named Mickey. Mickey was in a wheelchair and they both took a ride down! That was a crazy trip! Somehow they both survived it with no major injuries. Of course this was without the knowledge of any staff members! To go down steps in a wheelchair, you pop up and balance on the back wheels and do down front first. I have done it a number of times for single steps or curbs, but not a set of steps on my own.

The part of therapy I really enjoyed was walking outside. Again, I was fair game to be tripped and then have to get back up on my own, but I liked being outside, walking around the school, generally not just on the sidewalk also in the yard. This was on a very uneven lot, which makes walking harder, but that was part of the point: to learn to get better at walking. We would usually only do that when it was fairly nice out and since CCHS had school mostly year round, these walk would frequently take place during the summer. Often on my own, I would walk outside when I had free time, with a paperback book in my pocket. I would sit out on the lawn and read and lose track of time. Of course I tried to find places to sit where it would be easier to get back up. This would be, for example, part way up a hill. Then when I would get up to stand I would face up the hill and push up with my crutches, this made it easier because there was less distance between the ground and standing up.

One thing that you learn quickly when walking on crutches, is in order to keep your meetings with the ground or floor to a minimum, you need to watch where you are stepping at all times. People have often said that I appear to be depressed because I always look down as I walk. It has nothing to do with being depressed, but it has everything to do with making sure every step is precise. Each of my four feet, if you will, need to be placed carefully to avoid falling. Any wet spot on a tile, any little thing on the floor and one poorly placed crutch, I was on the ground. So this made me very conscious of always being very careful. My crutches became extensions of my arms. You can ask my brothers about how good I got with them. I would often reach with one of my crutches to turn on or off lights, even in full darkness. I remember one time when I was in high school and home for a break, I was sitting on a bar stool in the local pool hall watching some others play pool. One kid that was in my brother Mike's grade would often pick on me and he was one of the kids playing pool, and, like usual, making fun of me. I told him to knock it off, but he just laughed and mockingly said something about what was I going to do about it. I was holding my aircraft grade aluminum crutches in my arms as I often did, ready to get up any time. I looked down and gauged the distance between me and him and noted his crotch was the perfect distance. He was up against the pool table so would be hard to get out of the way. He saw my glance in that direction and held a pool cue cross ways just below his crotch, sneering at me saying, "Go ahead!" I said, "Are you going to pay for the broken pool cue?" He backed off quickly.

Part of my therapy do to polio and the variation in back muscles I developed a scoliosis. To help minimize that, at CCHS the therapist had me use a cart instead of a wheelchair. A cart is basically a wheelchair with the seat and the back removed, stretched out with a board with a cushion on it. It ends up about the height of a wheelchair's armrests. You lay flat on your stomach and push yourself with the big wheels, which in the case of the cart are the front wheels instead of the back as in a normal wheelchair. They are a bit of something to get used to, can be somewhat dangerous going downhill as they like to flip around if you get going to fast, and if you try to stop to fast, you can flip the thing over. But if you were good at it you could even pop a wheelie and balance on it like on a wheelchair. At home we didn't have any such thing but my dad put together a sort of one, using our wagon which Grandpa Sternhagen had built. He took it apart and strapped a sled on top of it. After taking the tongue that you normally pull the wagon off and with the sled on it backwards I would lay on it and use my hands on the ground to propel myself. The turning wheels that would normally be in the front were in the back, kind of like the cart. I could get going pretty decent when I would use it to go from our house to my Dad's gas station and back again on the sidewalk. Luckily my hands were already pretty much covered with heavy calluses from using my crutches all the time.

While I was at CCHS, I would have doctor's appointments at the Van Demark clinic. They would take us there normally at 1PM and then pick us up later in the afternoon. The place was normally packed and it could take a while to even get called into an exam room and then another wait until Dr. Van Demark got to you. If he happened to get an emergency call or something it could be a very long day and perhaps not get seen and have to come back probably the next week. I always was happy to have it take until at least three or so. As soon as we were all done, as sometimes it was more than just me from CCHS that day, they would call the school and let them know. One time I was actually done fairly early, they called the school and so I waited and waited. At seven or so when they were getting ready to lock up, I was still there. They called the school again, and the school had completely forgotten about me! I ended up sitting outside waiting until they could get me. I didn't get back to CCHS until almost eight that night. Of course I was starved as I never had any change for the vending machines at the clinic.

Dr. Van Demark to me was always bigger than life, though he was a fairly slight man in size. He was very no nonsense but always had an intelligent twinkle in his eye. He always seemed to know each of us completely just by sight. I remember one time my other doctor from the clinic, Dr.

Johnson, had done surgery on my foot and used some sort of surgical steel stitches. He wasn't there, so Dr. Van Demark was to take them out. He clipped the ends with wire cutters and tried to pull them out and couldn't! He was pulling away, and I was trying very hard not to scream as it was very painful. After a bit he gave up and had me come back the next day. They packed up the windows they had cut out of my cast and sent me back to CCHS where I spent a fairly painful night. The next day they took x-rays before I saw the doctor. He came in, looked at the x-rays, told me he had spoken with Dr. Johnson and figured out he done some sort of special knot on the inside. He slipped a surgical tool in, did something and quickly was able to get the stitches out.

Another time I had surgery on my left leg. Due to the polio it was turning out a bit and to correct it, they broke my leg and put pins in: one just below the knee and another just above the ankle. The cast had points sticking out from them. They then let it heal for a couple weeks, had me back into surgery and while I was knocked out they twisted my leg into position and put a new cast on. A couple weeks later when they were happy about the position and I was healing decently, they were to take the pins out, so a guy cut the cast where the pins were sticking out, which was very strange since the pins went through, and they used a vibrating saw to cut the casts. I could feel it vibrating my leg bones! It didn't hurt, just felt strange. I was worried that it would hurt when Dr. Van Demark pulled it out. I was remembering the incident with the steel stitches and didn't want a replay of that. He said it wouldn't hurt but just a bit as we can only feel on the surface of our skin not inside. He was right of course, and it was still an interesting time.

Chapter 12

Elementary school at CCHS went much better. There are just a few memorable items from fourth grade. Being able to take PE which included swimming, I enjoyed being in the water so much! No longer on the useless quest for the non-existent bingo marbles and industrial arts class, the fact that I was now able to take my books to my room when needed for homework made it easier to get most assignments in. It proved to be a better experience over all.

In fifth grade, some things started to change; there were only two other students in my class, and they girls. Since the classes were small at CCHS generally two grades were combined for at least home room activities. It was either the fourth and fifth combined or the fifth and sixth combined class that I started to shine somewhat. I remember getting my math done quicker than the others, then I would read or I would help the others with math, including coming up with problems for them to do and checking their work. At CCHS as well as all schools in SD at the time the Iowa Tests of Basic Skills was administered. It was often referred to as Iowa Basics. When I took them in fifth grade, I far outshined the others. I tested at eighth grade level in everything and at tenth grade level for reading comprehension. One of the clear advantages of a school like CCHS is that they can move students ahead if it seems fitting. The teachers all knew that it became problem if I was bored because like many kids I could be a bit disruptive, so they decided to have me skip sixth grade and move directly to seventh.

In seventh grade, I managed to keep up with most things rather well. The only thing I know I was and still am lacking in is some English skills, particularly related to sentence structure (my editor Jane Rokusek would say, "No kidding!"). In math I didn't miss a beat, in fact I recall one of the first times the teacher was going through long division and made an early mistake, I tried to correct her, which she did not take well, saying she was the teacher and I was there to learn and from then on I was to let her do the examples. I did this, noting along the way the mistakes she would make. At the end of a problem she would look it up in the back of her teacher manual and on the ones she had made mistakes on she would just say, "The manual must be wrong." I wouldn't let her off that easy though and would say, "No, look back in that step, you made a mistake there." This sure did not endear me to her at all. Needless to say, that teacher did not end up being a fan of mine. In fact more than once during my future school days she tried to do things to put road blocks in my way even after I was out of her both seventh and eighth grade classes. The other thing that my skipping sixth grade did was put me at the same grade level as my older brother by one year, Jim. I don't know how he felt about it, but I think he was okay with it, since we were in very different schools.

During this time I was also able to feed my passion for reading. The library at CCHS didn't have a huge inventory of books, but it had a variety to keep me interested! There was a set of biographies of early Americans, presidents such as George Washington, Thomas Jefferson and Abraham Lincoln. Also famous early American explorers like Daniel Boone, Davey Crocket and Kit Carson. I read them all, some many times over. The library would often get donated paperbacks and I got to a point where often I would read one of those a day. They were mostly westerns and I read them every chance I got.

Chapter 13
The Traveling Classroom

In the early summer of 1968 when I was in seventh grade we did something amazing, the traveling classroom. It was something they did every few years and at that time, even though it was supposed to be designed only for high school students, a few of us there that were not yet in high school got to go.

Traveling classroom bus 1955, which was about 12 years before my traveling classroom tour.

We traveled all around South Dakota on a Greyhound type bus. A great plus was if we had our own camera we were given some camera film, which was something exciting for me, since I consider myself a bit of a photography buff. If you couldn't find me reading a book you just had to look in the darkroom in the industrial arts area at CCHS. The bus left early on a Monday morning in May. Our first stop was actually where I live now in Brookings. After we visited SDSU and the Harvey Dunn gallery among other things, we ate lunch at the famous Nick's Hamburger Shop on main, where I remember having a hamburger, potato chips and a coke. We then headed north to Milbank. That is where I remember seeing cheese being made at a factory and also a quarry factory where they made tombstones. Milbank is where the day ended and we stayed in a motel there. Supper was at a civic club of some sort and the CCHS choir (not me!) had to sing for our supper wherever we went. We then headed to Ft. Sisseton, which had just started being a park, so there wasn't very much to see. Then on to Aberdeen where we had supper at another civic club but didn't really do much else for that night. We had to get up early to make it to the State Hospital and School in Redfield where they had awesome home baked bread and learned why we would never want to end up in a place like that. This hospital had originally been created as an asylum for the insane, or feeble minded. When we visited it was for those with severe mental disabilities and honestly not a very pleasant place. It really was more of a warehouse than anything else.

We also visited a Hutterite colony where we saw how they lived, even going inside one of their housing units. We learned that they ate as a community, but the women and men ate separately. They also had a very large ultra modern dairy operation that was in stark contrast to how they lived. I had visited the Mennonite colonies by Scotland with my parents and grandparents, so was a little familiar with how they lived.

Then to Mobridge, where we got to see and took pictures of the Missouri river and saw some Native American culture, then back over to Pierre where we spent the night and saw the State Capitol before crossing the Missouri at the Oahe Dam, then going west. We stopped at Wall Drug of course, taking more pictures and as I recall having buffalo burgers for lunch.

Wall is the gateway to the Badlands. There were some rest/visitor areas but something that I recall along the way was the general lack of handicapped facilities, yet somehow we managed. Often only those of us who could walk fairly well were able to go in at many attractions. After looking over the Badlands, we traveled on to Rapid City. We were able to stay there for three days. We were at a rather seedy motel that is now long gone as it was in the area of Rapid City that got flooded in 1972. While in the hills we of course went to Mt. Rushmore and it was a great moment when I got to see someone from my home town who was working there. I think it was one of the Rettedal boys. The chaperones liked to take photos of anyone we encountered on our trip that was connected with one of us. Smile, you're on CCHS camera! I remember the ride through the hills and Spearfish Canyon and the scenery being so full of high rock formations and so many trees. I also remember seeing snow in the ditches even though it was towards the end of May.

We then went to Hot Springs. Honestly I don't recall much of it, or what we saw. We were supposed to go to Evan's Plunge but it was closed for some reason, so we ended up just resting part of that day.

We then rode a long time until we stopped in Mitchell where we saw the world famous Corn Palace. The road trip didn't stop there as we continued on to Yankton in the same day. We ended up not passing through Scotland though (my hometown), which was a bit of a let down for me! At Yankton another group hosted a banquet for us. By this time of the trip the long bus rides and frequent motel stays were beginning to wear on us a bit, and things kind of become a blur in my memory. I do remember Gavin's Point Dam and thinking that was very cool to go inside and learn about the syncing of the turbines so that clocks would be properly synced. This early computerization interested me even back then. Our route home took us through Vermillion, but at that point it was just another town. Finally we were homeward bound back to Sioux Falls.

It really was a very cool thing to do, and something that obviously had an impact on me, as I recall much of it like it was yesterday thought it was 40 some years ago. It was a great expedition with our fellow CCHS students to be able to do something that got us out of the school and seeing and doing something enriching.

Seventh and eighth grade kind of blended together; they were both in the same room, same teacher. Just more advanced in eighth grade.

Chapter 14

High school was a bit different for us. George Washington Anderson was our main teacher. He was one of the smartest teachers I had ever known. Mr. Anderson was an older gentleman who had been at CCHS for some time. He taught English and math, among other things, and had a no nonsense approach in the classroom. In English we had 'themes' due every week. Themes were one page reports on an assigned topic. I was chronically behind on these. Luckily for me, he would accept book reports in place of 'themes' any time. When I got behind on them he would warn me on Friday that I had to have X number done by Monday or I would be in real trouble. I would usually wait until Sunday, go to the library, find the correct number of books that I had read, and quickly write the needed number of book reports. I always managed to get them done and in on time. As you remember, I was an avid reader and could always recall what any given book was about by simply looking at the title.

Mr. Anderson teaching. I am the one in the back on the left with of course my back to the camera.

The first class in the afternoon was math. Mr. Anderson would lecture for about a half hour. He would then give us our assignments for the next day and allow about one half of the class time to work on the assignments and ask questions. I would grab whatever book I was reading at the time and start reading, until the end of the class period. Since I didn't do my assignments at the designated time I'd then end up doing the assignment during our lunch break the next day and get it done just before class started. Yes, I know this was not very good study practice, but that is what I did. There was another student, Glen, who thought he was pretty sneaky, by getting the teacher to work out the harder problems on the board during the home work and question of the class period. Glen would then quickly copy that to his own paper. I was happily reading during this time, generally oblivious to what was going on. Glen thought he had really pulled one over on Mr. Anderson. At the end of the term, Mr. Anderson was talking about what grades he was going to give the students. Glen's average was just over 90 while mine was just under. He said he was going to give me an A and Glen a B, because he knew all my work was my own and that though Glen had thought he was being sneaky by getting him to do all the harder problems he was not able to figure out on his own, Mr. Anderson had seen right through him. Glen was incensed! He even went to the principal's office as soon as he could to complain. I was floored and of course very happy in spite of me reading during the end of math class. That moment had a strong influence on me when later, as a teacher myself, I would make judgment calls on grades. It also led me to name my first decent calculator, a Ti-30, George, in his honor—the very calculator I would later use to pass my FCC exam.

Mr. Anderson also had an interest in electronics and electricity. We later talked him into having a special topics class, which is part of what led me to taking electronics as a major in college. From that class I learned about basic electronics, schematic reading and things like that. I used this knowledge to fix the record player my folks had given me for Christmas, which ended up with a burned out transistor amplifier. Sometimes people donated old radios to the school for us to tinker on. Once I found one where the tuner didn't work, but the amp did. It was an old tube type and I figured out how to wire that to my record player and then from there to make a series, parallel speaker arrangement to blast my tunes around the dorm. The other kids thought it was great, the staff not so much.

While I was in high school, Mr. McCoy was moved into administration for a time. His absence in IA (industrial arts) was difficult for me. His replacement and I did not see eye to eye at all. It was my opinion that he was much more concerned with a nice neat work area than teaching me. Mr. McCoy allowed and encouraged me to explore many areas in IA that other students weren't interested in. The new teacher wanted us all doing the same things at the same time. This didn't work well with me and for a time the compromise they came up with was that during IA, I would paint the metal railing on the back patio. I managed to drag this project out for as long as possible. A project he did get me involved in was the construction of a special sandbox. I did a large part of the work on this, which was originally conceived and designed by Mr. McCoy before he was moved up to administration. This sand box was to be elevated so that kids in wheelchairs could wheel up to it and play in the sand. It was to have two levels, a lower level that fit little kid's wheelchairs and a higher one for the regular height wheelchairs. First we put it together in parts in the IA room, then it was taken back apart and moved to its permanent location, which was in the backyard of the school. One thing that kind of ticked me was, the teacher helped the seniors make a sign that listed them as the construction company, though they actually had nothing to do with the construction. I had a picture taken that showed me pretending to take a hand saw to that sign. In the end though the main thing was the sandbox turned out pretty good and was enjoyed by many students at CCHS.

Me showing what I think of the sign they made

Another project I was allowed to work on was to set up a Lionel train set that someone had donated so that it could be used by all the students. I spent a lot of time with this, using two 4x8 ¾" plywood sheets. I mounted the track in a simple square with a T crossing in between the sides. I did have fun with the project but was never able to get things stabilized enough to be able to be run by anyone. In the end he had me take it all apart. It was an older Lionel train. I don't know whatever happened to it, but am sure it would be worth a fair amount now, stabilized or not.

During the time that Mr. McCoy was in administration, somehow he got a Shetland pony named Trixie that was in foal for the school one summer. I along with a couple of other kids was in charge of taking care of it. The CCHS lot is rather large and what they had us do was stake the horse out and move it on a daily basis, so it kind of mowed the lawn.

Another task we had was picking up the droppings. This wasn't all that much fun, but we did it, putting them into many paper bags. I sure wish we had had the plastic grocery and garbage bags of today! She eventually gave birth to a colt that after a naming contest at the school was named Prince. There were a few issues along the way, at one time I tied her too close to a young tree and she proceeded to eat all the bark off it from the ground up to about 3'. Mr. McCoy had me paint it with some clear lacquer spray paint which actually did keep it alive but they ended up replacing it later anyway. As Prince got older he started to stray, running out into the street. He would come back at a whinny from Trixie but it was becoming a problem. He was too young to tie out, so someone had the idea of fencing them in, in the area outside the pool that had a wall on the north end and thick hedges on the west, the pool being on the east side, with garage doors that were most often closed. Only the south end needed to be fenced. Well, they got some metal fence posts and some clothes line rope. It looked great when we finished, but by morning they had walked right through it. We tried fixing but without rails or barbed wire no way it was going to work. Soon after that, it was decided they needed to find a new home for them on a farm somewhere.

For many years, the SDSU rodeo club had a fund raiser for the school. They would ride in relays from Brookings to CCHS, then at the edge of SF all mount up and ride to the school, usually coming in at about full gallop when they got right by the school. They would then give us rides around the lawn at the school. It was always a fun time, as I have loved horses since I was a kid. One time though it got to be more of a rodeo than planned. Someone was just helping me on a horse, when a wheelchair broke loose and ran in to the back legs of the horse, hitting it right above the hooves. It started bucking and I went for a pretty wild ride. Amazingly I managed to stay on it, though just barely. The girl whose horse it was, was of course mortified, and asked if I wanted to get off. I said no, I wanted to finish the ride. I knew if I didn't I would probably never get on another horse again. It went good after that, and I even made sure I got another ride on that horse later.

During vacation from CCHS I would be back home in Scotland. Those times always seemed too short. The summer one in August was always my favorite. When we lived in the house across from the Catholic Church, we would sometimes play army, mostly in the full block that was the church lot. One time I was left in a fox hole (ditch) furthest away from our house, while my brothers "borrowed" (took) both of my machine guns (crutches) and I ended making my way home unarmed in more ways than one. Though it was from the opposite corner of the block, I crawled until I got to the church building, then used the building to stand up and walked along the building until I got out front. Just across the street from our house, I was walking very slowly trying to get across the street and almost fell a couple times. I was almost exactly halfway across the street when my brother John showed up with one of my crutches and with that I was able to fairly easily make it to sit on the front steps of our house, until he recovered the other crutch for me.

The front steps of the house were also the location of some other experiences. One time we decided we needed to find a better way to kill these big black ants that were always by the steps. First we thought we would electrocute them. We used a lamp cord, put a button in the middle of it, and cut the ends off and soldiered the tips. One of us would put the electrodes on the ant and another would hit the button, no ants died, and luckily neither did we, as when we hit the button the fuse blew. That afternoon we went through pretty much every spare fuse in the house. The next day or so we decided to burn them, with lighter fluid. The only thing that ended up getting burned was my pant leg where it got fluid on it. Jim managed to get it out pretty quickly and I wasn't actually burned at all. One of our "nosey" neighbors called our mom and when we saw her coming down the street we all ran—well, they did; I went and tried to hide behind a tree on the way to the Scotland Motel that we shared backyards with. She was very mad and of course we got the typical "wait until your father gets home." I don't remember what all happened, grounded for life or something I am sure.

Chapter 15

When I was a junior I was able to attend a special summer program at the University of South Dakota at Springfield, or USD/S. It was called the STOP or Strategic Technical Opportunity Program. I was able to go to this because since I had skipped sixth grade and both my brother Jim and I were in the same grade, my folks thought it was ok if Jim also went. We went to the USD/S campus in the spring along with a friend of my brothers, Tim Cokely, to take a test. We all got accepted and starting in June, we got to take two-day introductory classes in different technical fields.

I took all I could in the electronics and computer field. This included courses on computers programming and a very simple computer that had to be programmed in binary, making it add. I got to spend our break time messing with it, where I put in the program to make it subtract, which is much more difficult than adding in binary. We had to use something called two's compliment. We also went over to USD in Vermillion and worked with the mainframe computer that was as big as my house and probably didn't do as much as a modern scientific calculator. We played tic tac toe on it! I was the only one that beat the computer! The programmer told me to do it again making the exact same moves and beat it exactly the same way again. After he noted the moves I used, he said he would program it to never let anyone beat it that way again. I tried again, and sure enough, it changed what it had previously done. We also worked with making punch cards, sometimes called IBM cards, but more correctly Hollerith cards. Interestingly enough it was almost the same time and I almost the same age as Bill Gates when he had his first contacts with computers.

I was in a wheelchair due to a recent surgery when I attended STOP. USD/S worked out reasonably well for me being in a wheelchair. Even though it was not specifically designed to be wheelchair friendly it mostly was simply by default accessible. The campus was fairly flat and because the university service vehicles needed to get around from building to building there was generally a decent way to get from place to place without having to jump curbs very often. I did sometimes have to go a long way out of my way to get where I needed to go, but I could always make it on my own.

The tech center at USD/Springfield was very wheelchair friendly

I remember when one teacher came back from a technical seminar. He put his briefcase up on his desk, saying that at the seminar they had been talking about making computers that would easily put that mainframe to shame; that it would be no bigger than his briefcase. We all laughed at such a theory! Of course that came to be true beyond our wildest imaginations!

There was also a course in machine tools that I took where we made bolts. I did very well in the welding course offered there, but didn't learn much beyond what I had already learned from Mr. McCoy. I also took a house wiring class, where we learned about wiring code and practiced wiring different switches and lighting arrangements.

We also went on a couple trips as part of the program. As I mentioned, I had recently had surgery so was in a cast on my left leg. I was in a wheelchair but I was able to walk some with my crutches and get in and out of the bus by myself. I made straps so that I could carry my crutches on the back of my wheelchair. One trip took us to the twin cities. We visited a Purina dog food plant and brewery, which I couldn't get into because of the steps. We also stopped at a manufacturing company, where I also couldn't go in because of no wheelchair access. A stop at the hydro-electric plant proved to be a bit of a let down, as it was far older and less advanced than the one at Gavin's Point that we visited in my previous trip with the traveling classroom.

All in all, this was a very good experience and I am glad I had the opportunity to attend. If I had not skipped sixth grade, it never would have been possible. At first it was only for juniors, and I am sure my folks would have only let me go because Jim went too. Another factor was that it was the last year they offered the program, which is too bad, as I think it really had a good impact on me and I ended up attending USD/Springfield for college.

Chapter 16

When I got back to CCHS from the STOP program, I noticed a strange transformation had come over many of my friends there. Some religious group had started coming to the school and converted many of them to their certain religious beliefs. They were going to bible study three and four times a week and of course my normal kid language was appalling to those students now. They were constantly telling me I needed to convert or I was going to hell and trying to show me their transformed ways. A very big controversial problem with this group was that they were telling my friends at school that they could pray away their disability and that if that didn't work it was because they didn't pray enough or believe enough. Eventually this religious group convinced a number of the students to even start refusing to go to therapy, telling them they would soon be cured so there was no need. As a result of this, the school eventually had to get a restraining order, to keep them off the grounds. They did so much more harm than good. I am pretty much a skeptic on that sort of thing and I think that even if I had been there when they came around, I would have seen them for what they were. I feel that there is nothing wrong with faith and prayer, but to rely on that type of 'therapy' is probably not the best idea.

Somewhere during this time in my life, I remember being in the restroom sitting on the toilet after supper one evening and contemplating life as one some times does on these occasions. I came to the realization that there would be no miracle in my case. There would be no cure and even if there might be, I could certainly not count on that. I needed to do whatever I could to make the most of what I had. That was a defining moment and since then I have for the most part followed that.

Chapter 17

While I was in high school, I had a great interest in photography and Mr. McCoy helped me a lot along the way, teaching me about framing photos, f-stops or how long the aperture is open for and other photography hints. A few of the staff members served as photographers for events and outings we had. Henry was one of them and of course Mr. McCoy. Eventually there came a time when all the regular photographers were out of town or busy and they had a volunteer appreciation and awards ceremony coming up and needed someone to take pictures during it. Both Mr. McCoy and Henry recommended me to do it. As I found out later all agreed with one nay vote: my old seventh and eighth grade teacher! She stated that since I was currently in a wheelchair I would be too low to take decent pictures, which is laughable since if you ever noticed very often photographers at events will be hunched or crouched down when they take pictures. In all actuality, it was easier to get a good picture without shaking or movement since you can rest your arms on the wheelchair ends up better than a tripod. I took the pictures and many were published in "Reflections," the school periodical. I went on to take many pictures; in fact, in one edition of "Reflections" all but one of the pictures was taken by me.

An all-call over the PA system can be very alarming, especially if your name is the one being called. An "all-call" is something they used for important things. In this case it was "All-Call, Mark Sternhagen report to the assistant director's office immediately!" The very one whom I had dealt with about smoking. I was very concerned as he was still the one in charge of discipline. I kept going over in my mind what could they possibly have caught me at? When I got to his office, I noticed he was on the phone. I also noticed the school's very expensive Polaroid camera was sitting on his desk along with a pile of film and flashbulbs. I was curious because he was not known as one who ever took pictures for the school. When he got off the phone, I think he realized I was nervous about what might be coming down, so the first thing he said was, "No, you are not in trouble for anything."

He then told me that they had a very important report that needed to be sent to Washington DC, next day mail by the end of that day, and they needed a bunch of pictures taken and all of the photographers were out of town. Mr. McCoy had told him I could do it. I was pretty much blown away. He gave me the camera, and the film etc, along with a list of about 20 different photos they needed taken. The teachers and other staff had all been informed that they were to cooperate with me fully and do whatever I said. If I needed more film or anything just let him know. It went great I got about ¾ of them taken when just before noon the camera died. They rushed it to Harold's and had it back ready to go by 1:30. I was able to get the pictures all taken and approved in time. It turns out this had a lot to do with the changes in the law that would take place. Pretty sure, it had to do with PL 94-192, The Education of All Handicapped Children's Act, and the funding that would eventually end up with a major expansion to CCHS.

Chapter 18

When I was in high school, a few of us decided we wanted to take the gun safety course required to get a hunting license. The course was offered free of charge at the old Washington High School in Sioux Falls. We badgered the staff until they finally agreed to let those of us who wanted to attend, including (gasp) any girls who wanted to go! This was one of the first things I was passionate about doing and worked hard at memorizing everything. When we took the test, there were five of us in the whole class that got 100%, and I was one of them. The ratio was about six "normal" students for every one from CCHS. Those who passed also got to go to a shooting range north of Sioux Falls on a Saturday and shoot clay pigeons, which was a lot of fun.

In South Dakota, the age to take Driver's Education was 14. At CCHS, they had driver's ed., but at CCHS it was not offered until you were 16. Again, I badgered them using the case that most other schools would allow students take it at 14 because that was the age you could get a learner's permit in South Dakota at that time. Mr. Johnson was the teacher and he was on my side. It was something else I was very passionate about. I ate the book up, reading and re-reading it, and it paid off as I was top scorer on all the tests.

When we started driving, we would go out in pairs. Of course we had to strictly follow all the rules of the road. I was paired with Richard Hettich and we would switch drivers each hour. I remember one time when we had switched drivers just off Cliff Avenue. When I got in, I was so excited to drive that I hit the gas a little extra and squealed the tires. Mr. Johnson wasn't too happy and gave me a stern warning. Another time we were driving down Philips Avenue and the light turned yellow just before we entered an intersection. I hit the brakes hard and Richard, who was sitting in the back seat without his seatbelt on—a big no no—almost ended up in the front seat. Mr.

Johnson told me that it was okay to go through yellow lights if you were that close and he really scolded Richard for not wearing his seat belt. While we were in the class, Mr. Johnson had to go to a seminar for driver's ed. teachers and had to take the driver's test as part of the seminar. When he returned, he said he bet no one in the class would do better than he did on the driver's test, bragging that he got 100%. I said I would do just as well. Unfortunately, when I took my test to get my restricted permit, I didn't realize that the South Dakota laws might be different than the ones in the driver's ed. manual I had memorized, so I didn't study the South Dakota Drivers Manual at all. I did pass, but I only got an 80%. The next year when I turned 16, I had gotten a copy of the South Dakota Drivers Manual, and of course memorized it and got 100%. I made sure to let Mr. Johnson know.

While I was in driver's ed., I didn't need to use hand controls as I could use my right leg well enough to drive the car they had. My dad's car on the other hand, though it was an automatic, it did not have power brakes. Not that I needed the power brakes so much, just that without power brakes the brake pedal is much higher and that was a problem. I had no money at all and my folks didn't have much either, so with Mr. McCoy's help I made a hand brake. It took a number of tries and failures, but in the end I was able to make one that worked very well and even including a hand dimmer switch. Driving with hand controls is not like you might think. With the hand brakes you tend to hit the brakes much harder than necessary, and it takes some getting used to after some very short stops.

When I was a senior in high school, we had a student teacher in geography. I thought she did a good job though to be honest I didn't really like her. She was kind of odd and rubbed me the wrong way. For some reason I was motivated to really try in that class from the beginning, even before she took over. I would read and re-read all the chapters to the point of complete memorization, just trying to do well on the tests. When she came she had plans to get us in touch with the different cultures we learned about from different geographical areas. When we studied China, we went to one of the only two authentic Chinese restaurants in Sioux Falls at the time. I was always kind of a picky eater and sadly I wouldn't even try most of the stuff they served us. Honestly, to me it all looked like someone had already eaten it and to use one of Mr. McCoy's sayings, "regurgitated it." In later years, I would actually try Chinese food and now many of their dishes are favorites of mine. We also went to a Mexican restaurant, where I was also skeptical, but did manage to have and enjoy a beef and bean burrito.

At the end of my freshman year, when the school year was winding down, the senior boys came up with the idea to sort of prank the office of Dr. Morrison. Since the seniors were somewhat less able than some of us younger guys and they were also seniors, we had some sort of obligation to do as they said, and we were enlisted to help. We managed to "borrow" a master key and since his office had a door that faced east it was fairly easy to sneak in and pretty much mess up his office. We brought in some plants and things from the front lobby, and scattered all the papers and books we could get our hands on in the office. The next morning when he came in early as he normally did, we were in our dorm and heard some shouting. At that point what seemed like such a great idea the night before all of a sudden didn't seem so good in the light of day.

Dr Morrison came down to our dorm, with a very grim look on his face and asked if we knew anything about his office. We all did very good at keeping straight faces as we said, "No we have idea what you are talking about." Well somehow it worked: he busted out laughing and all was good. So that night we decided it worked once, why not try again? This time we did the assistant director's office. Since he had come up as a physical therapist we decided to use that, and again gaining access to a master key, we got in to the therapy store room and took pretty much every extra wheelchair, crutch, brace and therapy device and crammed them into his office. His office had a side door that led into an office with a phone that we could use in the evening for local calls, which often meant repeatedly dialing the local rock radio station KISD phone number 336-1230 as I recall and requesting the latest hot song. This office access made it fairly easy to sneak the equipment into his office without being detected. The last things we put in were a couple wheelchairs that barely fit folded up, then we reached in and unfolded so the door barely opened. The assistant director was not known for having any sense of humor, but since we had pulled it on Dr. Morrison and he had laughed the assistant had little choice but to find it humorous.

We then waited a couple days and did Mr. McCoy's office. He had been moved up for a time into administration as the building manager, so in his office we put things from industrial arts where he had taught as well as general maintenance items, like mops and pails, including replacing his office chair with a commode with a plant in the bucket and tossed around some toilet paper for good measure. Of course Mr. McCoy had a good sense of humor so it went over fairly well.

We were often normal kids at CCHS. One time on a Sunday evening a number of us, including one kid who was unable to speak and used a board on his wheelchair where he pointed at the letters, were sitting in the front lobby. This was around the time when Woodstock had taken place and there was something called "The Fish Song" where they shouted, "Give me an F! Give me a U! Give me a..."—you get the picture. We decided to perform that in the front lobby. We were yelling it at the tops of our lungs while Gregg the kid who couldn't speak was point at the letters on his board. When the duty nurse, Mrs. Smith, who was probably one of the more church going of the nurses, came running up face as red as could be yelling, "What do you think you are doing?!" We were caught, no getting away from that. I had never seen her so mad. She said she was going to wash all our mouths out with soap! I said, "Then you will have wash Greggs hands out too." She burst out laughing and that was the end of it all.

Chapter 19

Our graduation took place on August 7, 1973. The six students in my graduating class were: Sherry Young, Dean Hansen, Richard Hettich, Greg Swanson, Joyce Perry, and myself. Richard was also a polio survivor. I am not positive, but I think Richard, Sherry, and I were the last polio survivors to graduate from CCHS. I was the youngest of the three, being only 17, since I had skipped sixth grade.

After the ceremony, Dean, who had a car, along with Sherry and I went to party. Well sort of. This was 1973, and there were not many convenience stores around. Also this was during the first OPEC oil crises, so most gas stations closed at 7PM. We didn't get away from our families until after 9. Dean had a small, cheap, travel-type tabletop BBQ grill and some hot dogs with buns, some chips, no ketchup or mustard, and had gotten a six-pack of beer in bottles. We had charcoal but no starter fluid so we drove around trying to find some place open to buy some. Finally we ended up at a truck stop on the north end of Sioux Falls by Interstate 90, where we bought a pop bottle of gasoline. I then wedged this bottle full of gasoline between my legs. We did find a cap, but it didn't go back on very well. We drove out in the country to find a spot to have our little party. We were not very familiar with the area and we managed to get lost more than once and ended up over in Iowa! We finally found a place for our 'party.' It had gotten cold out by then, so we decided to sit in the car while we tried to cook the hotdogs. We are lucky we didn't start the whole pasture we were parked in along with his car on fire! The hotdogs tasted like gas and the beer was warm, so it was a perfect graduation night.

We dropped Sherry off at the hotel where her family was staying at about 5AM. By that time we were almost out of gas. We happened to be on the west side of Sioux Falls, and had to wait at a truck stop on Interstate 29 that didn't open until

7AM. Once we were able to get gas, we drove to Dean's home by Utica, SD. I stayed there for a couple days. While I was there we played pool in Utica, did some target shooting and basically just hung out.

Chapter 20

There was a two-week period between the time I graduated from CCHS and when I started college at USD/S in Springfield, SD. I was familiar with the school from the STOP program I had attended the summer before my senior year. I had decided to major in electronic technology, for which they had a top program there. I will never forget the first day. After we got there and settled in, we all gathered in the Armory later in the afternoon; it was August, hot outside and inside as well with no A/C. They had as few lights on as possible but it was still brutally hot.

The University of South Dakota at Springfield

The department heads of our various majors were there to give the information we needed to get started for our classes. A memorable moment was when Jerry Sorenson, the head of the ET program, stood up on the bleachers and told us we had just decided on the best of all possible majors and that we could not have made a better choice. He basically was selling us on the major and did so in a loud and clear voice in case anyone from a different major was wavering. Mr. Sorenson was an inspirational teacher. He had ways of making you learn more than you really needed for tests. I always tried to model my later teaching somewhat after his style. When we later taught together, he would often say to me, "You are like a used car salesman." I would just smile and say, "I learned from the best."

A little local folklore about Jerry Sorenson. Jerry was a gun collector and the story was that one time he was cleaning a .22 pistol of his when "Gun Smoke" came on the TV. During the opening of the show, it would often start with Marshal Matt Dillon on the street in a fast draw gun fight. Well the story goes that Jerry decided to try and out-draw Matt Dillon, which he did and managed to shoot his TV! At the time I was at USD/S, there was a TV being worked on in the TV lab; they were replacing the picture tube, which had quite apparently been shot out. Whenever I would later ask Jerry about it, all he ever said was, "Arrgh! Where did you hear that?" He never said it didn't happen. Another bit about Jerry, later when he taught at SDSU in Brookings, he would often threaten to run naked to Volga. For example, "Op-Amps are as common as hydrogen atoms and if that's not true I will run naked to Volga!"

The first thing we did was take some tests including a fairly comprehensive one in electronics. Your outcome on that test determined where you started in the program, either in tech or pre-tech. If you were not well prepared they put you in pre-tech, where you would start with the very basics and also would have to take summer school the next summer to catch up, so by the following fall all were in the same place for the second year courses. I tested solidly in tech, which meant I was well prepared by CCHS, thanks mostly to Mr. McCoy and Mr. Anderson.

This is where the skipping sixth grade caught up with me; I was just not mature enough to be there at that time. I went from CCHS where every thing was structured and where cutting class was simply not an option. You knew when you would be getting up, what time every meal was and what time you would be in bed. If you were late or missing, they found you and right now! At USD/S it was completely different. No one seemed to care where you were or what you did. If you didn't make it to class, that was your problem. To make matters worse, though I was only 17 and drinking age for lower point or 3.2 beer in SD at the time was 18, most people assumed since I was in college I was 18. I was never once asked for an ID. The tap club in Springfield basically was in the business of making money off the college students and could care less who was being served, as long as they had the cash to pay for it. The one cop in town would only bother you if he really, really had to. I was without structure and rules for basically the first time in my life and I made the most of it. I am not proud of it, but it happened and it is part of where I am today.

The first fall semester went okay. I liked my electronics classes and made it to most of them and I managed to get to all the tests. But early on, I started missing my other classes a lot. English, which I had always hated, was first class for me to neglect. Soon even the math classes, which I had kind of liked, started being skipped. The real problem with missing a class here and there is that with each one you miss, it is easier to miss another. I had yet to learn the real key to success in college and that is pretty simple: GO TO CLASS.

I managed to survive the following spring semester, when it became even easier to skip in the next fall semester because the winter and snowy mess made it so difficult to get around. That didn't help motivate me to go to class more; in fact, my motivation was much less. I still managed to make it to most of my ET classes, but fewer and fewer of the others. My second year was awful! I made it to the tap club more than I made it to class. I even managed to completely miss a final exam for FM stereo circuits and got an F, one that I was never able to erase because later, when I went back to school, the course was never offered again. I had a couple other F's that I was later able to take care of, but by the end of my second year I had a 1.59 GPA and I left college by mutual agreement with them. Heck, I didn't need college; I knew all I needed to, right?

While I was at USD/S, I got my first car—a 65 Ford LTD. I bought it for $75 from my brother Mike, who was in the Air Force, stationed at Ellsworth Air Force base near Rapid City, SD. Mike had gotten a different car and so made me a deal. When he was home for a weekend, he took me and our youngest brother John back with him and we were going to drive my car back. When we got out there, it was evening and we were going to drive my car to go have something to eat. It started right up and I started backing out, but it killed. I tried restarting but it backfired and stared on fire! Luckily we were at the Air Base and they have a fantastic fire department! They were there and had it out fairly quickly. But there was some serious damage to the carburetor and some wiring. We ended up bringing Mike's car back to Scotland, with John driving since it was a stick shift and I cannot drive those. In the end it cost me another $125 to get it fixed and a few weeks later Mike brought it back to Scotland. I really liked that car after that and put a lot of miles on it.

While I was attending USD/S I would go home on weekends. Saturday nights, my brothers, some friends and I would to Groveland Park dance hall by Tyndall, SD. They didn't card anybody there; 14 year olds could even buy beer without any questions asked. Around the time that I parted ways with USD/S, I was at Groveland one Saturday night and had a few too many beers, when all the sudden I realized I was on the floor! Apparently I had fallen down. I got up and right then and there decided this was not for me. I had never really liked beer and drinking anyway. I had done it because everyone did and I just wanted to fit in. I realized that I am not everyone and I have rarely done things because everyone did. The main thing was the falling down. To me, being able to walk, even with my braces and crutches, was all important to me and anything that would take away from that was not worth it. Also being able to drive and have a car made me independent and that was also super important to me. I never have really had any alcohol to drink since that incident and I do not miss it in the least.

Chapter 21

The year I left USD/S, my dad got a new job as the superintendant at an apartment complex in Sioux Falls. He always had to work weekends, so his days off were during the week, when he would come back to Scotland. On many weekends, I would take my mom, who still did not drive, and my little sister Beth to Sioux Falls visit him. The job of being superintendant came with the perk of a fairly large apartment. That worked out very well for when we came for those visits. There was an outdoor pool there and Beth and I would go swimming when we visited during the summer. We also went to a few movies and we were able to see the Freedom Train, which was a traveling museum of the history of the United States.

Since I was no longer in school, I tried to open my own electronic repair shop. I worked at it, but there was already a well established shop in my home town of Scotland, where most of the local people went. I tried to get a job there but there was not enough work for me. My shop was out of my parent's house and it just did not do very well. My electronic ability was average and I was finding no one interested in hiring me. I kept busy at home with helping do some cooking and hauling my sister around.

Beth and I would sometimes go to my Uncle Tom's, who now lived on the Bickett grandparent's home farm. My grandparents had moved to live on my Aunt Margaret and Uncle Harold's farm near Crofton, Nebraska. Margaret is a nurse and Grandma had a number of health issues and Grandpa was retired.

Uncle Tom was a truck driver with two semis and when my brother Mike got out of the Air Force he went to work for Tom as a semi driver. Mike married Tammy in 1976 and they lived in the trailer house that Tom and Rose had lived in when they were first married on that same farmstead. Beth and I visited them very often. My brother Jim eventually started working as a mechanic at a service station a few miles from the farm. He stayed with Tom's family and I would stay with Mike and Tammy. I eventually moved into a trailer that was butted up against the original one. Once again, I tried opening an electronic repair shop, first on the farm, which did almost nothing, then in the town of Howard, SD. This only fared slightly better. I tried to find other jobs in electronics, but my ability was just average and nothing outstanding. I was starting to see that for someone like me, if my ability was the same as a 'normal' person, they were pretty much always going to hire that 'normal' person. All the laws and rules aside, that is just how it was, and in many cases still is.

While I lived there on the farm near Winfred I did all kinds of different farm things, including driving Tom's G John Deere tractor. The tractor, or as Tom called it 'Dear John,' had a hand clutch and if you had it in gear, you could use the clutch as a brake as well. It was fairly tall, but I could get up on it and down by myself fairly easy. I would even help clear snow with it during those South Dakota winters, where I learned a lot about snow removal and I guess that in some ways leads to my intolerance of poor snow removal.

While I was there my 65 Ford lost its water pump and I decided it was time to get something different. With Tom and Jim's help I found a 1969 Ford Torino GT, 390 cubic inch V8, a nice car, which I managed to throw a rod in after driving it for only two months. The best option was to find a different engine, which we did. I did as much of the work as possible. The replacement engine was at a salvage yard and to purchase it at the best price an engine block was needed to trade. It was decided to use the 352 cubic inch engine from my 1965 Ford instead of the 390 cubic inch from the 1969. In order to accomplish this, both engines needed to come out. I unbolted everything and got them ready to be removed. While I was running 'Dear John' and Jim doing the final work to get them pulled out we got it taken care of. It took me about a half day to get each engine ready to remove, and a half hour working with Jim to actually remove them. During my time there we actually did that on a number of vehicles for various reasons.

1969 Ford Torinio GT mine was white with black vinyl top

The replacement engine we got was a 351 cubic inch from a newer Ford car; the proper brackets didn't exist but Jim figured out how to make one and use one off a different car for the other. The exhaust didn't fit either, so he had to make a fairly complicated one that would cause all kinds of issues for most of the life of the car. He also had to shorten the driveshaft. He used a trick and got it working perfectly. It was a lot of work, but ended up with a really nice car, other than the exhaust system, which liked to break down fairly often. To fix it I would have to crawl underneath it and try and get things back together.

I got pretty close to the Bickett children while I lived on the farm and I have remained close to them ever since. I am as close to many of them today as I have ever been to anyone. Of course, I had a natural connection to Leo who ended up going to school in Howard for a time while I was living up there. It was right after Public Law 94-192 had changed things. This law encouraged—almost mandated—more mainstreaming of handicapped students into the public school system. Unfortunately, though there was a mandate to do it, many schools were not prepared. I know that Leo ended up facing many of the challenges there at Howard that I had in Scotland that eventually led to me attending CCHS. After a try at the public school, Leo went back to CCHS, which by then had changed its mission so he didn't fit in that well with the other students that were now attending. Most of them now had multiple handicaps. I guess I consider myself lucky that I missed that change over in the law and systems. I think over all it has been good, mostly for the public schools to have students with different needs mixed in their schools with them and they can see we are all just people, not someone to be feared and hated, but someone to get to know and be friends with.

Chapter 22

During this time I was receiving Supplemental Security Income (SSI), which is part of social security. It wasn't a lot of money, but I suppose enough to get by on and I suppose I could have lived on it the rest of my life. I am sure very few would have disagreed with me receiving SSI, but I always wanted to be more than that. I wanted to be able to earn a living like other people. It was nice to have the safety net and for many it is a life saver. But for me, it was more of a needed 'help along the way' income. I kept looking for jobs that I could do, applying where I thought there was any chance, with anything to do with electronics or something similar. The applying process always turned out the same: if I was just as qualified as the next 'normal' person, they would more than likely hire that next 'normal' person over me. I started realizing I could not be just as good as everyone else; I had to be better, probably noticeable better.

M-tron industry out of Yankton was expanding and I found out they were opening a branch in my home town of Scotland. I submitted an application through job service of South Dakota in Madison and took some sort of manual dexterity test there, which again, I rated average. I did get to have an interview with M-tron, so I decided to move back home and had high hopes of getting a job there. Well, when I got there for the interview in their shiny new building that the economic development group in Scotland had built for them, it turned out they had decided against expansion and there were no jobs available. They thanked me for coming to the interview and would keep my name on file in case anything came up at the Yankton plant or something. Of course nothing ever did.

Now I was back in Scotland, with no job or any prospect of one. I started helping more at home, doing a lot of the cooking and perfecting my cooking skills. I also started helping my mom at the Deluxe Dry Cleaners that she owned and operated in Scotland. I helped organize and tag the clothes when they came in. I would help with the dry cleaning and bagging of the cloths in the mornings and then clerk in the afternoons. My mom had a second job at Ray's Bar where she worked some afternoons and evenings, so my helping at the cleaners freed her up to work there or go home and get some things done or rest for her evening job.

I started making signs for the windows of the cleaners. There was a sign kit already there and the letters were the type that would glow in black or ultra violet light. We had a couple black lights in our junk collection at our house and I figured out a way to get them to light the sign at night. I started putting business ads about dry cleaning and how efficient it was in taking care of your special clothing items. Often I'd just put cute little sayings on the sign. I think it had a positive impact on business and it didn't really cost anything.

There was a small safe in the building that the previous owner, then deceased, had left locked and no one knew the combination. One day when I didn't have a lot to do, I started working on it and was I able to figure out the combination and get it open! I discovered that is was empty except for the paper with the safe combination on it! But it was a fun puzzle to solve and I can add 'safe cracker' to my resume.

Chapter 23

I think it was that fall while I was reading the paper. I saw an advertisement for night classes at USD/S. The one that struck me was FCC rules and regulations. It was the time of communicating with CB Radios and there were lots of them out there, not only in semi trucks but also in cars and homes. To legally work on them at that time, you had to have an FCC license and that class was the class that would prepare you to take the license exam. It was only two credits and was at night, so I could still help Mom at the cleaners and only one night a week. I was planning on paying for it myself, but when I told Mom about it she offered to pay the tuition. I went to the campus at Springfield and even though when I had left USD/S years before not in good standing, night classes fit into a slightly different category, so there wasn't a problem with me taking it.

I was now determined to do well! I had learned along the way how much I didn't know and that I couldn't be just as good as the next guy. I had to be better, much better, if possible. I had to work harder and prove to everyone, mostly myself at this point, that I could do it, that I could be successful. I made sure I made it to every class, even when the roads were treacherous. I got there early and made sure I was ready. Every week we took tests. These tests were practice tests for the FCC exam. We would then would go over the test from the previous week and work on problems.

The book was a very big, thick question & answer manual. I basically memorized the whole thing. I read it over and over and over doing all the practice problems, answering all the questions. This was long before the internet, so there wasn't a place to look things up. My math skills were poor and I was very sorry I had ditched most of my math classes when I had attended USD/S the first time. I ended up having to memorize equations in different forms because my algebra was weak and it had been way too long since I had tried to learn it. For the fall semester the instructor gave everyone an incomplete, because to get an 'A' you had to pass the actual FCC exam that was to be held in Sioux Falls that next April.

I signed up for the spring semester in the advanced FCC night course and also started volunteering at the college radio station, KSTI, with goals towards both engineering and radio announcing. I managed to get hired on as a DJ one day a week for the late afternoon shift on the same day that I would have night class. To say 'hired on' is a bit misleading: I didn't get paid, but had the position. The teacher for the night class was the communications electronics teacher and he was also in charge of the radio station. So this worked out very well! I was never late, never missed a shift or a class and all that worked in my favor.

In April, I went to Sioux Falls to take the FCC exam. I got there early, got myself ready and relaxed. The process was that you would take the second class exam and if you passed that, you got to take the third class exam; if you didn't pass that, you didn't get your second class license, but could try the third again within a certain time frame. The teacher had drilled into us that even though the third class test was pretty easy, we needed to make sure we had the material for that down as well. The second class exam is very hard. There was a lot of math and it was by far the more important of the two.

I was very nervous. I had extra batteries for my TI-30 calculator 'George' because, as the teacher said, if your calculator dies, you go with it. I did the best I could. There were a lot of math problems and my math was still very weak. When I finished and took the test to the FCC examiner, she counted up the ones correct: 75 out of 100! This was the exact score needed to pass. She then counted the answers which were incorrect just to be sure and there it was: 75%! This was not a great score, but to me, it was everything, I PASSED!

Even with my weak math skills. I then nervously took the third class and got 100%. so I was in! I had my second class FCC license! Since I was there, I also took the first class exam, but was not prepared for it at all and although I got a 62 on it and didn't pass it, at this point it didn't really matter.

Passing the test meant I got an A for both the FCC courses I had taken. It also proved that my 75% was nothing to sneeze at, as over half the class did not pass at all. I planned to study over the summer and take the first class again in the fall, but that summer the rules changed. They eliminated the first and second class licensure but later they would bring them both back as a general class license—meaning if you held a second class license, you could apply for and get a life time general class license. I did this and hold that general class license, allowing me to work on any and all transmitters other than RADAR. There is no doubt in my mind that I would have been able to pass the first if I had been given the chance.

The second class radiotelephone license had been required to work on transmitters of any size, from CD radio to most radio stations and some TV stations. Before they changed the law, it was a very big deal to have this license and also very important. A person with a license had to be either onsite or monitoring most broadcast stations whenever they were broadcasting. They were also responsible for making sure the station was on correct frequency and at proper power at all times. Accurate logs were kept, although that person did not have to personally take all the readings. Everything that went out over the air was the responsibility of the engineer with at least a second class license. Including if for example someone used restricted or foul language, they were, or in my case I would have been the one fined, not the person who actually said it. When they changed the law requiring a licensed person to be responsible at all times, all of that changed as well, which is part of what has led to the more lax control of language on the air today. For example, in the past if you said a word like "shit" on the air, it was a $10,000 fine; now it is ignored.

Chapter 24

That summer I volunteered to work at the radio station on campus. I didn't take any classes, but I had contacted SD Voc-Rehab and talked them into paying for classes for the next year. I was signed up for nine credits for upcoming fall semester. I was mainly the only person at the station, and we were only on the air a few hours during the day. I learned a lot during that time. I always just assumed since it was a small college station very few people would be listening anyway. I pretended that few was actually none, as that made it easier to just do the job and not worry about who might hear me make a mistake. I also studied for my first class exam until I found out it was no longer offered due to changes in the law.

That summer I had apparently made a good impression on the teacher. He was the same teacher who had taught the FCC classes. When fall came he happened to be the teacher for most of my classes, plus he was also my advisor. When I went in the day before classes started, he told me that the person who was supposed to be the station manager for that year had dropped out over the summer along with the program director, as well as the chief engineer were no longer enrolled. Both the station manager and the chief engineer needed to hold at least a second class license, no longer the FCC requirement, but this was the school's requirement as well as his requirement. He said he had someone else in mind for chief engineer, which was a relief as I was not yet ready for that. That fall, I was scheduled to take the courses that would prepare me for that, such as communications systems and resonating systems. He said due to my work that summer, if I wanted to try the station manager position, it was mine! I was shocked! He normally preferred a work study student because he felt if they were paid, they were more likely to do a good job. I was not on a work study program, but he felt I was truly the person for the job.

There were many students who had been at the station longer than me and also some others who had passed the second class license exam, but since I had worked that summer five days a week and approximately five hours a day, there were few who had more on air time or experience than I did. This meant I would also be the president of the student radio club by default.

I think it was also that fall that my brother Mike had quit truck driving and moved back to Scotland and was hired as the city night police officer. He took advantage of the GI Bill and also started taking classes at USD/S in carpentry. We ended up in a couple of classes together and would often drive to Springfield together.

The fall semester went well. My goal was to try and better my GPA every semester and during that semester I got all B's. The spring semester, however, presented a problem. The communications class and lab went well, but a class called resonating systems had a lot of complicated formulas to deal with; it was much too difficult for me and once again my lack of math skills proved to be a problem. I then learned the second lesson about college: when you are not going to make it in a class, get out while you can! I dropped the class and focused on the rest of my classes and got mostly A's that semester. That summer I took some self study math classes and in the fall, college algebra. By the next spring I retook resonating systems. This time I was ready and did very well. In fact, I was almost at the top of the class and that is saying a lot as there were some very sharp students in the class.

The final exam in that second semester resonating system class taught me a lot about myself and also about tests and test taking that would later impact me as a teacher. I had always been a good test taker. I had in my mind that a test was basically just an opportunity to get out of class early. I would often do better than I had a right to and was good at doing exactly as well as I needed to, like in the FCC exam. I felt I normally had very little test anxiety and really found the idea a bit ridiculous that it would actually matter.

In the resonating as well as the communications classes, the teacher used a points system, with points being awarded for tests, home work, and midterm tests. The midterm had higher points and the final carried most points of all. Depending upon how many points you had earned would show what grade you received for the semester. With his system, it took only 75% to get an A, but he gave very few A's. His theory was think or sink. The tests were very hard, all a lot like the FCC exams. I had done very well this time through resonating two and when I got to the final I was only some 50 points away from an A for my final grade out of a possible 500 points for the final exam. So I didn't really study at all, I just glanced over the material. I knew I could probably get the 50 points and an A by just circling C for all the multiple choice questions.

I decided that although I wouldn't really study, I would try my best, which I did for the most part, but I did skip one problem. This was not because it was too hard or I didn't know how to do it, but because I knew it would take about 20 minutes and cut into that whole get out early idea I always had. I ended up getting the second highest score in the class, which I did not expect at all. As it turns out, I did much better with no pressure at all and apparently I had much more test anxiety than I had ever thought. It really changed how I looked at tests and in particular when I would give tests as a teacher it was something I kept in mind. It was also something I would relate to students to try and get them to do better on tests. The idea of a test should not be how many students you can trip up with tricky questions. The idea should really be to find out if they are learning the material. I know that many teachers I have taught with along the way do not agree with that and feel that for a test to be of any value it must be hard.

Chapter 25

During this period of time in college, there were a couple of things that happened that got me to thinking more and more about my future. One of the things that happened was through another Scotland resident. Greg Zweifel, who was a few years older than me, started attending USD/S as a freshman in the electronic technology (ET) program. We started driving together when our schedules worked out and also ended up in a couple of math classes together. We would push each other to do better. I would sometimes help him with his introductory electronics classes, and he is the first person to mention I should think about being a teacher.

The other thing that happened was I took my first computer programming course in the Pascal programming language. I found I had a real connection with computers. I really enjoyed the class and would often have the program we had just been assigned to write, written by the time class was over! I would then try to get to one of the only seven computer terminals available at USD/S. Some of these were mostly for office use, but they would roll them out into the halls for student use after the offices closed. The terminals were off the main frame located at the USD/Vermillion campus; actually, it was in the same area as that mainframe I had worked on while in the STOP program.

I would get my program typed in. Then I had to submit it and wait for it to process. Sometimes it would take a few seconds, but often it would take a few minutes or sometimes even an hour or more. It was best if you didn't log off while you were waiting, besides I always wanted to find out if it had errors or had compiled properly. It didn't make sense to work on the program until you found out if there were any errors or problems when complied and run by the mainframe. While I was waiting, I would often read the manual for the system, which included a lot of sample programs written in JCL, or

Job Control Language. This was the language that controlled the mainframe. I learned a lot about computers from reading the manual during these waits. Since I was a mere student, I had very limited rights on the system, but with JCL that didn't matter. If you happened to know the right things to type in, the computer had little choice but to do it. I did a lot of experimentations that might be considered hacking in this day and age, but in the end that is part of what has helped me become knowledgeable about computers. I believe you have to have a little bit of the hacker mentality to truly dig in to what the computer system is all about. People have asked me how I got so proficient in computers and I always tell them that I am a poor speller and have awful penmanship and that computers are good at both. I am a self-taught touch typist and even back then, with main frames, there was a rudimentary spell checker, although it only worked when you sent the file to a special program and then it only sent back a list of misspelled words and what line that word was in the document. You then had to find the proper spelling on your own and replace the word.

In the second semester of computer science, I really got into the depths of computers even more. The programs were much more complicated, which I didn't mind at all. They were more of a challenge and this was what I had a passion for! I also started helping others in the lower level class who were having problems with their programs. I found how true the old saying "to truly learn a subject, teach it" actually was, by helping others. I got a much deeper understanding of computer programming, by finding their errors and I learned much more than I would by simply fixing my own errors. This led me to think even more about teaching and led to my decision to pursue two degrees at the same time.

There is a federal mandate in place that states in order for Vo-Tech schools to get federal funding, the state they are located in needs to have in place a four-year school where a degree in Vocational Technical Teacher Education or VTTE is available. This degree is to educate teachers for the Vo-Techs. In South Dakota at the time, USD/S was the designated institution. I decided to pursue a BSE (Bachelor of Science in Education) in VTTE degree at the same time that I was working on my BST (Bachelor of Science in Technology) in electronics. Since I had completed most of the BST degree, I put the remaining classes that were in that major on hold. That decision had to do with Voc-Rehab. They would stop paying for classes once I got a BS degree in anything. I talked to my Voc-Rehab counselor about it and he recommended getting both degrees at the same time was the best direction to take. Getting both degrees at the same time would make me the most employable. My goal was to teach electronics in a Vo-Tech in South Dakota, or the surrounding area. Another option was to teach computer science.

While I was in the second semester of computer programming one of the last programs we had to write was called the towers of Hanoi. There are various other names for it. Basically you have three towers, or poles and different size discs that must be moved from the first tower to the last with certain rules. This program used something called recursion, where the program literally calls itself. The problem with recursion is that it takes a lot of computer memory and the amount allotted to students would only allow something like four discs before it crashed the program. Using the JCL programming that I had learned by sitting and waiting at the terminals, I figured out how to get more space. I learned that the more discs you try to use, the amount of space goes up exponentially. I pushed the process and tried 11 disks! I ended up overloading the whole mainframe and crashed the entire state system. The computer science teacher was understanding but did say to never do that again. So I was more careful in the future.

I was able to keep working with computers; writing programs, some for myself, but also for the radio station. I wrote a program that would use the record library information that was already cataloged in the system, to come up with playlists using 100 songs for the week and generating five different playlists. These were to be used for certain timeslots or radio shows during the week, to keep the DJs from just playing the songs they liked over and over. It was fairly complicated, so unfortunately I had to be the one to run it. I found out that writing a program to do something is not the hard part, the hard part is writing it so that anyone can use that program so it do what it was designed for. Sometimes called "idiot proofing," probably at least 95% of programming is making it easy enough for the basic person to run it, and only about 5% actually writing a program to perform a task. In today's world that might be closer to 99% and 1%.

I also took a class in Apple BASIC, which was my first experience with a personal type computer. After the rigorous programming of Pascal and JCL on the main frame, I found the Apple simplistic and more of a toy really than anything. It was cute and neat, but that was about it. Also, when I first opened one up, from a purely technical perspective, I thought they were poorly made, perhaps even purposely designed to not last and with the need to be replaced. They have improved somewhat over the years. I did great in class, though I hated it when we had to do flow charts. I considered them a waste of time. You were supposed to make a flow chart and then write your program based on the flow chart; I did it the other way around. I wrote the programs, got them all fine-tuned, and then made the flowcharts. I got high marks on my flowcharts. They were always perfect and the best in the class because they always matched the program exactly.

I also took a statistics course. I found it interesting, as we were going through things like standard deviations. I started writing a program to calculate different statistics as I was going along basically just because I found it interesting. As we would learn something new, I would add it to the program. It was a very crude program; however, I learned a lot programming it. If it is true that to truly learn something you need to teach it, that also applies to programming, because to write a program to do something you need to fully understand the process needed to get from the given input to the desired output and to do it correctly every time.

At midterm in the statistic class, we were given a two-part test. The first part was the normal multiple choice, and the second part we were to take home over the weekend. It was a list of 100 scores for a test and we were to find all the statistics about the test scores. The instructor gave us a list of statistics we were to find based on these test scores. Well, the program that I had been working on was far from finished, but I thought, what the heck and spent about 10 hours that weekend finishing the program. During the weekend I got the program to the point where I could type in the list of scores he had given us and it would produce a list of the statistics that he wanted. I figured I better make sure he knew I had written the program, so I handed in the source code along with the sheet with my answers on it.

Oddly enough, the statistics teacher was not into computers at all, so he asked the computer science teacher if he thought I had actually written the program or just copied it from another source. The computer science teacher, who knew me well, said he was positive I had written it myself. The only problem with my answers were that they were more accurate and the statistics teacher actually found that he had an error in the answer key because it conflicted with my results. He rechecked and it turned out that I was right! This was one of the first times my computer skills, in fact perhaps in a way my computer gift, was shown to be above average. Not just a bit above average but noticeably above average! I received an A for the course; I could have quit coming the second half of the semester and I am pretty sure I would have still gotten an A.

Where did this computer gift I seemed to have come from? Partly, I think, from having polio and being handicapped. I always had to calculate things, looking for ways around obstacles; planning every move carefully, even where each of my crutches and feet would end up with every step. If I did not calculate and plan each step, it meant I would soon end up on the ground. I had to develop patience and perseverance. I had to keep trying. For example, when I would fall down in a slippery area and no one was around to help, I had no choice but to figure out how to get back up. This took careful planning. Computers are like that—not so much on the user level, but on the lowest levels, at the machine level. Every step must be precise, one thing out of place and the whole thing crashes. You also need to be able to look at the big picture, getting from point A to point B and at the same time making sure to cover all the little tiny steps in between. Perhaps part of it is an actual gift. I don't know that, but I do know that I started finding that I had a far above average ability to understand computers.

Chapter 26

I continued to work at KSTI, although I was no longer station manager. Normally the station manager was changed every year or so to give others a chance at it. I was happy to move back to just being an announcer or DJ. I would still spend a lot of time there and as I mentioned made playlists for different programs, like classic rock, country hour throughout the week. I also trained a number of up and coming announcers or DJs along the way. Working at the radio station had many advantages; you always knew everything that was going on, which would prove to be important.

In the fall of 1983, when I was well on my way to completing both of my degrees, everything started to change. The South Dakota governor, Bill Janklow at that time decided he wanted a minimum security prison. Part of the politics for it was to use USD/S either as that facility or perhaps it was just a ploy to get people on board with the idea of building his prison. Governor Janklow proposed the idea of closing USD/S and turning it into a prison. Perhaps the mistake the administration at USD/S made was when they lobbied against this proposal, they pointed out that education should be more important than incarceration and that it was perhaps foolish, even stupid to think otherwise. Basically, they were saying that whoever came up with this idea was foolish or stupid. That attitude pretty much doomed the school. The governor did not like being called foolish or stupid! I personally believe that at that point, there was no turning back. He was going to close the place. If he couldn't turn it into a prison, he would turn it into a toxic or nuclear waste site! The fight was on and we had no real chance of winning it. He was pretty much a no nonsense, my way or the highway type person that got his way—which of course can be good or bad: if the bully is on your side possibly good; but in this case, not so much.

We were all up in arms over this decision and working at the radio station got to be exciting. We did whatever we could to get information about the situation. We soon were able to find out that even our own administration at USD/S was not telling us the whole story. More than once we got calls from them asking where we got our information. All we would say is, "Is it true?" and then they would just hang up. I learned a lot of invaluable lessons during that time, about politics in general and in South Dakota specifically.

At one point the governor visited USD/S supposedly to explain things. We found out that while that was the 'official' agenda, he in fact wouldn't mind if, when he visited, there was a demonstration or riot so that he could point and say, "See, they are really no better than the convicts I want to send here anyway." The radio station, because of our technical knowhow and equipment, was in charge of the public gathering that he was to speak at in the Armory. We had all our people ready with microphones around the building with the orders that if anyone got unruly they would shut off that microphone and move on to someone else while allowing that person to calm down. Since I had the most experience, I was designated as technical director at the station itself, running the board and controlling what went out over the air. We had also talked the speech and forensics teacher into doing a possible interview with the governor after his meeting with students. The interview would be in the production room and I would be in control of that from the control room.

The meeting went well, no riots and everyone was calm and respectful. The governor said nothing new. He just reiterated his plan. At the last minute he agreed to the interview at the radio station. We were prepared for that and the interview went well. He did say a couple things that he would later deny he had said and we did of course have it all on tape. But he was the governor so in the end it was all meaningless. It was 1984 and the thoughts and comparisons with George Orwell's book were at the top of my mind: big brother got what he wanted.

There came an occasion that my computer science teacher caught me in the hall and mentioned that the administrators for the mainframe computer system in Vermillion had sent him a message that the state computer system had seemed to have developed a sense of humor. It had been observed that random things were popping up on terminals all over the state, such as jokes about the governor, often with spelling errors. They wondered how the system had developed this sense of humor and yet somehow lost the ability to spell. My teacher said he was sure I knew nothing about it but that they had said as long as it stopped they would not pursue the matter further. It stopped.

That next semester we tried to go forward with business as usual, taking the classes we normally would have. The bill that was proposed to shut USD/S down, also the one to turn it into a prison, went down in defeat. We knew it wasn't over until the end of the session. We did send reporters to Pierre a number of times to cover the discussion. On the surface it seemed like the school was not going to close and the administration was saying all would turn out well for USD/S. Through our other sources we were not getting that same message. There seemed to be a last minute ploy or plan coming from the governor's office that could change everything and that maybe he was purposely waiting until the last minute to make that happen. Even though the original bills had been completely killed, it was past the time for new bills to be proposed. South Dakota has something termed "hog housing," which means that they can gut a current bill and change it around to contain anything they choose at the last minute. This was named after something to do with a hog house that was proposed at one time at SDSU.

On the last Saturday in February 1984, they were working on doing just that. We found out late Friday and sent a reporter to Pierre. I ended up coming back to Springfield on that Saturday to be on the air by 7 o'clock in the morning even though we normally wouldn't even be on the air on Saturday until noon. I played stacks and stacks of records and was on the phone with the reporter most of the day, waiting for something to happen. I kept telling people what little we knew between playing records I was the only one around and hadn't brought lunch with me. The union which was just across the same building was closed on Saturdays. Sometime in the afternoon, I put an album on and while listening the whole time in my car, I drove down to the local Casey's and grabbed a quick lunch. It seemed strange when I went into Casey's: they had a little radio playing in the background and I noticed it was playing the same song as I was just listening to in my car! Then it dawned on me, they were listening to our campus station! So much for the whole assumption 'no one ever listens so I don't have to worry about sounding like an idiot' idea I had always kept in the back my mind when I was on the air.

By the end of the day, they voted to close USD/S and turn it into a minimum security prison, unless a suitable buyer could be found that would keep it as a university. The last suggested alternative turned out to be not much more than a scheme to keep the current students from trashing or defacing the campus out of anger and frustration. The governor made sure he torpedoed or stopped any attempts by anyone to purchase the campus as it was. USD/S was closed down at the end of the semester and turned into a prison. The day they voted also happened to be the day my Grandma Bickett died and two days later, on Monday, February 27, I turned 28 years old.

The students filed a class action suit since we were not permitted to finish our degree programs, which was a breach of contract. It took some time going through the system and in the end the judge ruled that we were right. However, since it was the state and the governor there would be no reward other than the knowledge that he had gone about things the wrong way. The state of course, had the right to close the university, but they also had a legal obligation to see to it that the current students could finish their programs.

On a sad note, a solid half of the students decided the heck with it all and left college never to return. As for myself, I took another approach. I was like, screw me? Well screw you! I am going to succeed one way or another.

Chapter 27

The South Dakota Board of Regents did say we could transfer to any South Dakota BOR school and finish our degrees. There was a guarantee that all credits would transfer. What they didn't tell us was that yes they would transfer, but not necessarily into any other major. I decide to not wait around to see if they moved my programs to any other university, or if there was some talk of the ET program being set up at all. I had figured they would have to do something with the Vocational Technical Teacher Education or VTTE program or shut down the Vo-Techs as well. I decided I wasn't going to wait and applied to USD/V and applied for whatever financial aid I could. I then rented an apartment in Vermillion and started summer school.

I moved to Vermillion about two weeks before summer school started. I also decided I needed to seriously consider losing weight. My Grandma Bickett was really the driving factor behind that. She had always been on me about my weight, including the last time I had visited her in the hospital. She had a weight problem most of her life as well and ended up with diabetes. I know she was afraid I would end up with the same diagnosis, as there is diabetes on both sides of my family. A couple years before I had moved back to Scotland, I quit smoking. I just decided I was going to quit and so I did. I only quit once and haven't ever smoked since! I quit just like I had done with drinking, though I don't think I was really ever dependent on drinking.

I thought I could perhaps do the same thing to cure the weight problem, but it turned out to be a bad plan. I didn't eat for three days straight and then was so starved by that time that I felt like eating anything in sight! But I did manage to control myself and made some chicken in the Wearever Chicken Bucket, a pressure cooking deep fryer that drastically reduces the amount of fat absorbed, I had gotten from Grandma

Bickett. After eating I decided what I would do: I would only eat supper, since I had found it difficult to sleep when I was so hungry. I would start my day with a single piece of dry toast with my coffee in the morning. I would not eat lunch then eat a fairly square meal for supper—not a great big meal, but something decent. That worked out for me. I was about 230 when I started, and by the end of the summer I was under 200. I slowly eased back into eating more regular meals and I finally did get down to about 150 pounds. I haven't quite been able to stay at that, but have been able to mostly maintain my weight at about 165 or 175, which I think is a much better, more stable place to be. Remember, as a polio survivor exercising to lose weight is not a good idea and could lead to other more serious problems. So I actually lost the weight totally by dieting. I am not saying I suggest this diet, but I am saying it worked for me with Grandma Bickett and the Chicken Bucket's help.

This crash diet did come back to haunt me a bit the following spring. I had been visiting both DSU in Madison and SDSU in Brookings. Since I had one day a week without classes, that was my opportunity to start looking at other schools. The morning after the day of the two college visits, I got up as usual, went to the bathroom, came out and fainted! I was really scared! I thought it was the post polio syndrome I had heard about! That is a scary situation where you can end up back as you were at the worst of your polio. For me, that was in an iron lung, only able to move my right wrist and turn my head slightly. I ended up in the hospital where they ran a bunch of tests, including a 24-hour heart monitor. It turned out it was partly from dehydration and partly due to my rapid weight loss. After that I balanced out my meals better.

While I was at USD/V, some classes were interesting and some not so much. I will admit I had a bit of a chip on my shoulder after the whole mess at USD/S but I was determined to succeed whatever it took. That summer I took a couple of different computer courses and calculus I. I did okay in calc, and pulled a B. The first computer course I took was a BASIC programming course, this time on the IBM PC, which I liked far better than the Apple I had done BASIC on previously. It was a solid computer and the programming was easily adaptable from the Pascal I had learned on the mainframe at USD/S. The other course was programming in Assembly language. The instructor did everything he could to make it as hard as possible. I did okay with the programs, but the class and testing were much more difficult to deal with. During the summer, courses are compressed in such a way that a day is what you would usually cover in a week. The first test we had was in the evening after a full day of classes. I was the first one to complete the test and that was after 3½ hours! The programs on the test were insane and there were questions on the test that I had not even a clue about let alone ever heard of. I felt I had been very diligent in my preparation and when the instructor finally handed back the test I asked him about those questions that I had no clue about. He said they were from chapters coming up and that any decent student would be reading ahead. I decided to drop the class. I knew he was not a very good teacher. Perhaps he was a good programmer but not a good teacher. I really didn't need the class as it turned out. The only thing I really took away from the class was some idea of what not to do as a teacher.

The rest of my year at USD/V went well. I took a number of education classes. I felt all of those were good. The professors did a good job and I learned a lot. Some of the other classes I took were not all that great. I took a chemistry class where the teacher said the first day, something like, "I am not a teacher because I want to be; I am a chemist, and had an accident and was exposed to some chemicals, so I can no longer work as a chemist, so I decided to teach." He may have been a good chemist but an awful teacher.

That fall I found out that the college had finally evaluated my transcript and while they would accept all my credits, they would be mostly credited as electives. This meant that I was basically starting over as a first semester sophomore. Another problem was that, since I had been pursuing two degrees, I had too many overall credits. There was a limit to how many credits you could have without getting a degree and still get any kind of financial aid. All my credits made this impossible to complete all the credits I needed to get for a secondary teaching degree and still get financial aid. That is when I decided I needed to look at other opportunities and chemistry was not required for any of those. Even though I had taken the midterm, I dropped the course. The scene on the day after the midterm was kind of funny. There was a line of sad-faced students lining up to either drop this chemistry class or see what they could do to pass after the disaster of a midterm. When it was my turn to see the professor, he looked at my test and said I had done quite well. He was sure I would be able to pass his class. I just said I am changing my major so wanted drop it anyway. He did seem a bit shocked.

Western civilization was another class I took. I like history and liked learning about it, but again, I did have not the best teacher. I took copious amounts of notes, read all the books, yet on the first test I didn't do very well. I couldn't figure out what I was doing wrong until I found out he had study sessions before each test, where he basically told those attending what was going to be on the test and what he wanted for answers. If you didn't go to them you were basically screwed. I did stay with that class because I liked the subject and managed to pull a B without going to his stupid study sessions. Again, my gain in this class was what not to do as a teacher more than anything.

One thing I noticed at USD/V and had some at USD/S, was that if I signed up for a class that was on an upper floor of a building without an elevator, when I actually got to the first meeting of the class it would have been moved to a first floor classroom. Also, I am a pre-planner so I would scout out the buildings I had classes in before the first class. This way I could see where the handicapped parking was. Often when I would show up for the first day, there would be an extra handicapped spot and the class would have been moved to a ground floor classroom. I found out years later that the campus actually were tracking the classes I was taking and made sure they were making an extra effort to accommodate me, without my knowledge. Looking back, I really appreciate that and wish that SDSU had a similar view of how to best accommodate similar needs. At SDSU I fought tooth and nail for my rights as a handicapped person from my first day to my last on campus. It was a breakthrough of USD/S, USD/V and also DSU to do the accommodating without doing more to make me feel handicapped.

The year at USD/V was mostly uneventful. I was kind of bitter about the whole event of the closing USD/S, but still did reasonably well in my classes. Along the way I found out they had moved both of my majors to other state schools. The electronics program had moved to SDSU in Brookings, SD and the VTTE program to the then Dakota State College (DSC), now DSU in Madison, SD. The two schools are about 45 miles apart and I decided to see about going to both schools at the same time and see if I could still graduate with both degrees and under the credit max for financial aid. I stuck out the whole year at USD/V because I had signed a one year lease on my apartment in Vermillion.

Chapter 28

When I left Vermillion that summer, I moved to Madison, SD. My Uncle Tom's oldest daughter, Cathy Steinmetz and her husband Doug had an older trailer house in Madison that they were looking to rent out. This was perfect for me so I rented it from them. I started taking summer classes at DSU and began working with my VTTE advisor to plan out how I could complete my VTTE degree and do my student teaching in the EET program that had moved from USD/S to SDSU. At the same time I applied to SDSU so I could also complete the few credits I needed for my EET degree. I ended up going to both schools for a year! I graduated from both colleges the following May (that was a busy weekend!): on Saturday from SDSU with a Bachelor of Science in Electronic Engineering Technology and on that Sunday I graduated from DSU with a Bachelor of Science in Education in Vocational Technical Teacher Education. I also took the National Teachers Exam at DSU, and did very well, testing in 95th percentile for professional knowledge and well above the national average in all other areas.

While at DSU I took as many classes in PC computer use as I could. This included: word processing, spreadsheet and database programs, all of which I excelled in and went much further in than the classes required. DSU was a leader in up and coming technology far ahead of SDSU.

I applied for and got in to graduate school at SDSU in the Masters of Science in Industrial Management (MSIM) program in the College of Engineering. My overall GPA was 2.95, even though I had 4.0 for all at both SDSU and DSU. I was still making up for the poor showing I had my first years at USD/S and not doing great but average at USD/V. My first semester in grad school finally pushed me over 3.0 overall.

At SDSU my computer knowledge really started paying off. SDSU was way behind DSU in PC user type programs such as spreadsheets. I took a business management course where a mainframe simulation program was used. We were divided up into groups and each group was a company selling shoes. We had to fill out and turn in prepared forms. They put the info into the simulation and then they would hand back how we did. I built a spreadsheet that would calculate and make recommendations for the form. It would also allow me to project numbers using 'what if' scenarios. I brought my print-outs to the group and we decided to try turning them in as is. The professor was very impressed and gave us extra points the first time we turned them in. By the end of the class, I had fine-tuned the spreadsheet to not only let me predict how we would do, but how the other groups would do as well. It was almost like cheating, but it wasn't cheating. It was using technology to beat technology. I could see the future was not with mainframes but with PCs. I had used my little spreadsheet to beat a big bad mainframe at its own game.

I also was accepted as a Graduate Teaching Assistant or GTA. This is a sort of paid position, not well paid, but better than nothing, plus it meant I got a reasonable break on tuition. Since I was planning on being a teacher, it was a natural fit. I ended up teaching in the EET department, which included a number of labs and also classes under the direction of the full professor. After the first year I ended up teaching a number of classes with one of the two regular professors listed as teacher of record, but me being completely responsible for the classes. Since we had many of the former students that had been in the system at USD/S, where there had been five full-time instructors and no funds for additional full-time faculty, so they used GTAs like me.

EET was housed in Solberg Hall, at that time an older engineering building, and was under the College of Engineering.

Solberg had a lot of stairs. In fact it was not possible to get very far into Solberg without stairs. Offices and a couple classrooms were on the second floor, the labs on the third. I ended up having to go up and down those stairs a lot.

I continued to live in Madison and drive every day to Brookings. I also let them know at DSU that I would be interested in teaching there if they had any classes I might be qualified to teach. DSU was a fairly small school and I had managed to make some good contacts there, I knew almost all the teachers and I also got to know most of the IT support and technical staff. This was a rich environment to learn a lot and get exposed to a lot of different software. I started working with desktop publishing and also some programs to make different and in my opinion some pretty cool fonts. This was before that was common; in fact, that was one of the things that cemented me getting the GTA job. The department head for General Engineering or GE, where the EET department was located, was Dr. Duane Sanders. When I met him to be interviewed for the job, he had my resume which showed I had this fancy font program to highlight things, for example, listing my degrees in an old English font, very much like the font used on the actual degrees. I remember he said, "If we don't hire you would you still do my daughter's wedding announcements?" He was kidding of course, but I knew I had made a point. What I could do with computers was far beyond the average person. Shortly after I had started in the GTA program, he had me install my first hard drive ever, in his secretary's computer—an AT&T IBM compatible desktop.

Chapter 29

I was willing to try and learn almost anything that had to do with computers. I had a natural ability to figure out where the installation programs were wrong, which was actually about 95% of the time. If there was the least a small error in the procedure, I could most likely figure it out quickly. Soon after I got started at SDSU there was a demand out in the electronic industry for students with experience with PC based CADD, most specifically Autocad. At the time, SDSU was deeply entrenched in mainframe-based CADD, but I could see where the future was and it was not in mainframes, so I quickly offered to teach a special topics course in Autocad. Coincidently, at about that same time, a local electronic manufacturing company that Dr. Sanders, by then the Dean of Engineering, had direct ties to, Daktronics, needed someone to help them get quickly into Autocad and they hired me with Dr. Sanders' recommendation, to teach a night class in Autocad. This went very well, and by summer they had me teaching a couple sections of that class and they also wondered if I could teach Pagemaker, a desktop publishing program. While I had done some desktop publishing, I had used Ventura, a rival of Pagemaker, and very different program, but of course I said I would.

The problem was, I didn't have a computer and I needed access to one to be able to prepare for the classes during the summer. There was a small startup computer company in Madison called Dakota Micro Management. I knew the owners and they were very busy with their regular jobs during the day. I offered to watch the phones during those daytime business hours, if I could have access to the office computer while I was there so I could prepare for my night classes. I said they wouldn't have to pay me anything since Daktronics was paying me.

This worked out very well for me and for them. They had a client with a very expensive daisywheel type printer. This type of printer is actually an electronic typewriter that can hook up to a computer for printing very high quality printing, like the type required in legal documents. In fact the client was a law office and one of the owners for Dakota Micro had sold them a number of PCs to replace a proprietary system they had been using. Part of the agreement was that they would get this printer set up to work with the PCs. So far, the two owners of Dakota Micro, who were supposedly hardware people, had worked on it and gotten nowhere. Mike, the other owner who was strictly software, asked if I would have a look since the lawyers were wondering about the progress of this project. I said sure and started messing with it. I had it printing nonsense almost right away, something they had never been able to do. I figured out that someone had altered the circuit board— probably whoever sold them the proprietary system, to keep them from being able to use it just like we were trying to. In under an hour I had it all figured out and printing perfectly. My electronic background coupled with my programming and software skills made me far better than the next guy. I went with Mike the next day to Clear Lake, SD, where we installed the printer for the client, the now Gunderson Law firm.

On a Friday in July of that year, I got a call from Dr. Bruce White, the head of the business and information systems dept at DSU. They had an instructor get called away for a family emergency and had no one to finish teaching the course in BASIC he was currently teaching. Would I be interested in stepping in and teaching it? It didn't conflict with my teaching at Daktronics, so I said sure, and then he said, "By the way, can you start on Monday?" Of course that was not a problem. It went very well; it was an 8-week course and I taught the last four weeks of it. At the end Dr. White said they were going to try and offer some night classes down in Sioux Falls that fall and if I was interested in the computer concepts class I could have it. By then I was mostly done teaching at Daktronics, as they had most of their workers up to speed. So I ended up teaching two nights a week in Sioux Falls, taking classes and teaching at SDSU and working at Dakota Micro. It was a lot of driving, but I really like to drive so I was happy to do it.

I was still working without compensation at Dakota Micro. They were going through some growing pains and eventually Mike bought the other two owners out and then I did end up getting paid. I was able to learn a lot, mostly through trial and error. I am extremely cautious and careful about backups when working on computers. Though I learned a lot from mistakes, I never lost any important data. Again, my patience and perseverance, acquired from the many years of having to work around my handicap, paid off. I quickly went from good at computers to very good at computers, both hardware and software. I also did well with the third and most important part of computers, people.

Partly because of teaching and partly because of my background, but also due to my solid very much above average understanding of how computers worked, I was able to work well with the customers and I always tried to not talk down to them. I tried to never make them feel stupid for not knowing something, or for making mistakes. In the back of my mind I have always kept the thought, "If they knew what I know about computers, what would they need me for?" With that as my 'motto,' I would always try to explain things and help them understand so perhaps they wouldn't make the same mistake again. As someone once told me after a particularly messy server upgrade, I pretty much always did it with a smile. My main rule has always been to treat computers like computers, and people like people.

One of my first experiences with Microsoft Windows was at Daktronics in Brookings, I was teaching a couple of night classes for them at the time. When I came in about 5PM to get ready for my class, I was asked to go have a look at a computer that wouldn't print. They had something that had to print from that computer and it had to go out that night. I get to the computer and their resident expert, an electrical engineer, had it taken all apart and then had left saying he didn't know. I put it back together, hooked everything up, and asked if they had tried to print from any programs other than Windows. At that time windows ran under DOS; it was not the overriding operating system it is now, but just another program. They told me no one had tried to print other than from Pagemaker which ran under Windows. I first went into WordPerfect under DOS and it printed fine. One of the first things to do when troubleshooting is to isolate the problem to either hardware or software. They had spent hours messing with hardware when it turned out it was a software issue. I ended up re-installing the Windows 3.0 and Pagemaker on the system and everything worked as good as new.

When I was in graduate school at SDSU, I was taking a course in Management of Information systems, taught by a professor in computer science. At the time I was living in Madison, working at Dakota Micro Management pretty much full-time as well as teaching at SDUS in EET as a GTA at 49% (just under 50% so they didn't have to pay benefits). Since it was a graduate class the professor wanted to tour some places that were ahead on information systems. He suggested Dakota State (DSU) in Madison, and wondered if anyone had a connection there. I said I did and told him just to tell me when he wanted to tour and I would set it up. He also asked about Daktronics. I again said I could organize that too, but another student said he worked there and he wanted to, so after mentioning that I knew a LOT of people that worked there, I dropped it.

I talked to a teacher, Tom Farrell, at DSU that owed me a few favors for computer things I had helped with, including speaking to a couple of classes, and he set up an excellent tour including refreshments. My teacher was very impressed and kept thanking me. A couple weeks later we had the Daktronics tour, given by the student from the class. It wasn't very impressive except for the fact that about every third person that met us along the way said, "Hi Mark, what are you doing out here?" including Frank Kurtenbach one of the main people at Daktronics who came up to me and asked if I could look at one of their computers. A computer science intern had decided that this IBM clone type AT (Advanced Technology) computer needed its internal battery replaced, even though it was not causing a problem. In those days when you replaced the battery it lost the system setup. The most critical part of that was the hard drive, and you had to know what you were doing and have the right software to do the setup. They had neither. This computer had their complete customer list; the only current copy and the most recent backup was from many months back and they had made significant additions to it since then, so many man hours of work would be lost if they couldn't get it. I took one look and said I had the right software in my car, went out and got it, came in, booted, did the set ups, had it back to normal and was able to rejoin the tour just as it was about finished.

Chapter 30

I continued to live in Cathy and Doug's old trailer house in Madison. They had moved to Minnesota for Doug's job as an electrical lineman and eventually we made an agreement where I purchased it for the rent I was paying and had been paying. It was small and had walls that were made of 2x2's with little to no insulation, but it worked for me. Tom's second oldest daughter, Mary, helped me fix it up quite a bit! We managed to get some nice carpet remnants and installed them for like $100. We then took all the cabinets apart and stained them a dark color with lighter colored trim. It was amazing how nice we were able to get it to look. I really appreciated all her help. Later, when she started college at DSU, she would come to the trailer during the day between classes. Sometimes she would come and have me help with her homework. By that time, I was no longer teaching the classes for DSU. I was still in grad school and was hired on a more full-time basis at SDSU.

Mary ended up taking BASIC programming and she would call and ask for my help with writing her programs, usually the day before they were due. I would try and lead her to figure it out on her own, which she proved capable of doing. Also, I helped her study for her tests. A couple years later as she was helping clean out some things at my house, she found the info I had kept from that summer that I had taught it, including all the test keys, which they were still using. Of course I had known that those were still there, but I wanted her to learn it so hadn't mentioned it.

Mary and I have been very close every since then and we have helped each other out many times. Mary was in the National Guard and got called up for active duty in the first Gulf War. While she was gone I wrote her very often and sent her care packages which consisted mostly of blueberry Pop Tarts. Since I worked at the computer store we would get hard drives packed in very good packing foam; this made good packing for sending packages on to her. Also, I found out that the packing foam along with some duct tape made some decent pillows in the Gulf.

I kept working at Dakota Micro, now a full-time paid position. We got into networking and more systems support. I was also still teaching at SDSU and my department had decided to have me develop some computer systems type classes and eventually a major emphasis in networking and support. I strongly felt it was important to keep my hands in the real world of computer support while developing and teaching courses in the topic. There is no teacher like real experience. While the lab can simulate things, it is just not the same. In the real world you have to stay ahead of things, while in the lab not as much and in the real world you have to worry about things that matter to make the system better. In the classroom it is easy to get stuck in your ways and not grow. I cannot imagine that working very well with computers. When working with computers, it can truly be said you cannot step in the same river twice. Things are constantly changing: what was the right thing to do yesterday, or even this morning, maybe isn't this afternoon.

I remember the day Mary got back from the Gulf. It was a July fourth weekend and since her unit was out of Aberdeen, that is where they were set to return to. I headed to Aberdeen from Madison and since I had to drop some computer items off at a small town along the way, I took a bit of a different route than you would usually take. Mary's family was traveling to Aberdeen as well. It was a strange coincidence that as I was coming from the south, I met her brother Pat at a four way stop pulling a trailer coming from the east. I followed him into town, though I am not sure he knew where the Armory was because he drove right past it and I turned in the parking lot. It just seemed odd we had met at that four way stop in Webster. I knew he was probably going up, but I had no idea when. It also shows how lucky some people can be! Tom and his family were coming and planning on camping up there over the weekend. Even though they had not made reservations and it was the fourth of July weekend, he had his usual luck and managed to get a couple of nice spots by a lake. I didn't stay with them. I was mainly there to welcome Mary and her unit back home! Mary came over to my place in Madison that Sunday night after they got back and we drove around for hours while she told all about her experiences in the Gulf. She also borrowed my Bronco II for a few days. I had two vehicles at the time, the Bronco and a Chevy Berretta GT, so it was not a problem to lend her some wheels.

That was the year Mike sold out Dakota Micro to a guy who had been working there as his office manager. As it turns out this guy had been creating some friction by playing the rest of us against Mike and vice versa. As soon as he took over he made some changes, and not for the better! He also tried to play us against each other, but it didn't work. One of the first things he did was to come and tell me that the other tech Eric thought I was being paid too much and that I should take a pay cut. I flatly said no and that if he cut my pay a dime I would quit. I knew how good I was and what I was worth. Eric was good too, but we both knew he was learning much more from me than I from him. When Eric got back I made sure we went on a service call together and asked him flat out if he had said anything; he said he had not. I am positive he was telling me the truth and the other guy was lying. I knew after that incident my days there would be numbered and started making plans to move on.

While I still liked to drive, driving to Brookings every day was getting tedious, not to mention hard on cars. The hard fact was that what I was making at Dakota Micro was paying my car expenses. I did the math and figured I could get an apartment in Brookings and maybe start my own small company, and even if I just made a few bucks a month I would come out a little ahead and not have to drive all the time. Of course, I talked it over with Mary. As it turned out, she was going back to DSU and was going to have a baby. She was interested in my mobile home, so we were able to work out a deal for her to live there and pay utilities and not have to pay rent if she would help me find a place in Brookings and help me move. My plan was to give notice that I would be quitting the end of July and move after my two weeks were up. That way I could make some money during the summer as we only got paid during the school year at SDSU.

When I turned in my resignation, the owner had a fit! I was ready to leave that day after his reaction! I still had two weeks of vacation time coming and I told him that he had to honor that. Even if he happened to say no, I knew he probably couldn't just let me go as we had an important network to install in that time frame and Eric had already quit. The newly hired guy was nowhere near ready to do it on his own and, to make matters worse, this owner was the only person I ever knew who was truly un-trainable on computers and completely clueless on networks. He ran to his lawyer, who apparently told him to suck it up and also told him that I had every right to quit at any time with proper notice. He also informed him that he had to pay me what he owed me. I did all my work and then some the last two weeks while employed there as well as teaching Bob, the new guy, as much as possible.

Chapter 31

The day after I finished working at Dakota Micro, I officially started Computers Networks Systems and Support; later it was incorporated. I did my first network install, as the new company, the following weekend with another one-person computer company. We did a few jobs together, but I quickly figured out he was using me for my knowledge and ability and was looking to make some quick bucks, so I soon severed that relationship.

I also moved to Brookings with the help of Mary and her brothers, Pat, Dennis, and Tim. They were all of great help. The boys were attending SDSU so that worked out very well. Mary's youngest sister, Rita, was also going to attend SDSU starting that next fall. Mary lived in the trailer house in Madison, with her baby, Shane.

On a Saturday that fall while I was getting gas at the Amoco station, I noticed that there was some sort of the business sale going on. As I was pumping gas, Dennis Evenson, from the Clear Lake Law Office I had worked with while at Dakota Micro Madison, happened to be there for the sale and came up to me. We exchanged friendly greetings and then he asked me if I was still working on computers. I simply gave him my card and he called the following Monday. As it turns out, Dakota Micro wasn't doing very well in the costumer service area, especially for clients like themselves. There was a printer in their office that they had sold them and they were not able to get it to work properly. Dennis asked if I would be willing to come to Clear Lake and take a look at it, which of course I jumped at the opportunity to do. Within the next couple of days I drove to his office and got it working right away. They have been one of my better and friendlier clients ever since.

I did start some minor advertising right away, small ads in the paper and shopper. I also did some radio ads. I found my radio experience at KSTI was definitely a good thing. I wrote and cut my own ads, generally only needing one take to get them right. I didn't expect to get many new clients from Brookings at first, but it finally paid off about a year later when some clients finally started contacting me. By that time Mary had moved to White with Shane and Shane's father (later to be her husband John). Mary helped me with the computer store which was run out of my apartment and I helped her get ready for her wedding. With Mary's help I eventually opened up a small computer store in Brookings. I hired college students, including Mary of course, Rita, and a number of Rita's friends. Mary's brother Dennis also worked for me occasionally and Pat helped getting the place I had rented ready. The college workers were by far my best workers. I couldn't pay a lot, but was very flexible with hours etc. One job I usually had one of them do was to go with me on service calls. This was mostly to be my legs and that worked out very well.

My first store was in a little strip mall on sixth street and later I moved into the University Mall. We eventually got very busy and I hired a full-time tech and office manager. I hated doing the office stuff, so I thought a full-time office manager was a good idea. It turned out to not really be such a good idea after all. The full-time tech didn't work out that well either, as he was nowhere near my level and really did not learn well from mistakes. I got a lot busier but unfortunately the overhead rose just as quickly and in some cases quicker than I could financially manage. During the years that I had a store front, I often worked 16-hour days between the store and teaching at SDSU full time but I never really seemed to get ahead. After a number of years I was kind of forced to close the store front, which has been a good thing. I still do computer consulting along with computer and network support mainly for businesses out of my house. I stay about as busy as I want to be with it and it keeps me up to date with my computer knowledge.

I found that hiring college students for the office staff seemed to work the best, though it was a bit of a nightmare trying to schedule a number of part-time workers. Initially doing payroll would take the better part of an afternoon, until I finally broke down and bought Quick Pay. I had a couple of part-time tech students from college. Brian Tonsoger who had worked with me at Dakota Micro in Madison was now attending SDSU in the EET program and worked for me a few hours a week. When he graduated I thought I needed a full-time tech and a former classmate from USD/Springfield was in the area and we cut a deal. Initially when I changed the business to a corporation he was to buy in with me matching but that didn't end up happening. I later found that I did better with part-time workers as techs as well. I had a number of high school students from the area. They normally found me and I had decent success. They were more energetic and wanted to learn. I also allowed them access to my technical area during off times. They would often spend many hours in the evening working on their projects. I would always answer any questions they had, sometimes directly like when they were working on a job and efficiency pays better than none. Often when they would ask me questions about their own projects, I would answer with another question to get them to think it out on their own. Most of them grew a lot technically while working for me. I also worked very hard at trying to get them to work well with customers. A real stand out was Garrett Fields.

Garrett came to work for me in kind of an interesting way. He was going to Sioux Valley High School in Volga, SD. Sioux Valley was almost exclusively an Apple computer based district. Garrett had transferred from out of state when his dad moved to Volga to teach at SDSU. At the time the Governor of SD had put some money into funding networking for local high schools using prison labor, ironically trained at the Springfield prison. Garrett was trying to get the school to use the money they had allocated to connect up to the network in

an efficient manner, he had gotten a copy of the school's plan
and budget and came over to ask me my thoughts. I took a
look at the plans and right away felt they were not doing a
very good job of using the money. They had contacted a
computer store in Watertown and they had recommended a
very large expensive server. The school did not need a large
expensive server—they barely needed a server at all. What
they needed were workstations. The price of the server would
have provided for a decent lab of about 20 computers. I ended
up talking a lot with Garrett about it. We put together a plan
that made much better use of the funds. Unfortunately the
school board refused to even consider Garrett's plan. But from
that meeting Garrett ended up asking about a job and turned
out to be one of the best workers I have had. Technically he
was the best I ever had, in some ways better than me. With the
customers he had an easy disarming way about him, not in the
least threatening. He never made the customers feel ignorant,
which is something many tech and technical sales people tend
to do. Garrett never did anything like that. I very often had
good compliment about him from customers.

I had other workers who customers would tell me they never
wanted touching their computers again. They were technically
good but had no people skills. I always tried to get them to
work better with people. I normally had some success, but I
also know how hard that can be. I often found that with
students as well, some of the best technically were just plain
awful with people skills. Why is that? I think it has something
to do with the fact that they choose areas like IT support
because they like computers and technology and are far more
comfortable with computers and technology. Perhaps they
lack the empathy needed to understand people's frustration
with the technology. I feel that once again in this area being
handicapped is a bit of an advantage: my natural inclination as
a nerd is to not to work well with people and to also lack
empathy, but being handicapped it tends to also bring out the

empathy in people. You get used to observing people, to being an observer rather than a participant.

Chapter 32

I was up to the academic challenge at SDSU in all the classes I needed to take to finally get my master's degree. It took me a little longer than some students since I was working all the time. I was then hired full time as an instructor in EET.

A very big challenge with my job at SDSU was the lack of handicapped accessibility. I had never been a complainer. Most of my life I would find a way to work around things. The lack of snow removal was always hard to deal with and became a major frustration for me. I would carry several bags of sidewalk ice melt in my car all the time, sometimes going through two or three 10Lbs bags a week. I would spread it in front of me as I walked. When I first started there they actually pushed the snow up into the handicapped spots. It appeared to me that the snow removal crew made some assumption that there weren't that many handicapped individuals, so the spots were only filling some sort of legal requirement anyway. Of course one of the reasons there have always been so few handicapped individuals at SDSU is the lack of those accommodations. Sometimes, it gave you the feeling that maybe someone did not want you there, a bit like the feeling I had when attending grade school in Scotland. I do feel and have been told that I should have been more vocal about the problems. I would sometimes complain a bit, but rarely loud enough to the right people. It really is not in my nature to try and make people make special accommodations for me. I probably should have looked at the bigger picture; that as a faculty member it was my duty to bring the inadequacy to light. I will admit, it has improved some and is better now, but there is a very long way to go. Part of it is their attitude and failure to address the handicapped population. The city of Brookings, along with many businesses in the city, unfortunately, take their cues on this from SDSU. I will say the University Mall is an exception. During the time that I had a store there, they did an exemplary job of snow removal.

When I first started teaching in the EET department, there was a major emphasis in electronic communications that already had an instructor and a major emphasis in video or television repair that also already had an instructor. I taught mostly lower- or middle-level classes along with labs for classes that others taught during the first couple years. The television repair industry was quickly fading and with all my computer knowledge it was proposed that I would create some computer classes. Later, the classes needed for a major emphasis in computer and network support would replace the television repair emphasis, and communications would also be dropped as a major emphasis. Eventually only a single communications course existed, which was taught by others. I taught most of the computer-related courses from digital electronics, which is the bits and bytes that lead to computers, to micro processing, which is how computers work. This was probably the hardest class I taught and also the one that made most students the most frustrated. The frustration has to do with the fact that computers do all these wonderful almost magical things, but under it all they are extremely simple stupid machines. No smarter than a light switch that turns on a light. Often people think it can't be that simple. The reality is computers accomplish what they do by incredibly simple steps, many simple, precise steps, that are done very quickly and that makes it seem like there is so much more.

My most popular class was computer systems. In this class we talked about how the PC computers work. This included covering all the hardware and how it works together, along with operating systems and software. As part of this class we would often build computers. These computers would then be used in other labs in the department. I would put together a list of parts and go through the state bidding processes and hopefully everything would come together so the students could assemble them before the end of the semester. A couple times we had to cut it pretty close and at least once the parts didn't make it in time to meet the deadline. The nice thing about this was it was real hands on and I was there to check before they powered up to make sure they did it right. A few times they didn't power up correctly and we ended up destroying parts, but that is part of the learning process.

I also taught two senior semesters in networking and support as the part the major emphasis in computers. We reached a point in the networking classes where each student would have two computers to use for networking and then they would all have their own network. Each student would install all the software. One semester was normally Novell networking and the other semester Microsoft networking. We were moving towards more Microsoft and other options and less Novell.

One thing I did in the computer labs was to be somewhat hands off. My office was connected to the lab so it was a little easier to ignore them and let them figure things out on their own. Since this was a lab, it wasn't a situation where it had to work or the company couldn't work or faced down time. I would try and give them hints as to what to try. I know from experience, you learn so much more by figuring it out on your own, than if you would just be given an easy answer. Sometimes it would almost drive me nuts. I knew the answer and it would have been so much easier for me to just do it, or tell them exactly what to do, but then what would they learn?

In all the computer classes I taught, I tried hard to work on attitude as much as technical know how. So many working in IT are good with computers, but their people skills are a bit lacking. I feel that while being technically competent is important, perhaps what is more important is how you deal with people. Many students who go into technical fields like IT do so in part because they deal better with machines or things than they do with people. Also, there is often an arrogance that can come with having a tremendous amount of power because he who controls computers controls the world.

I feel it is not in their best interest to be so arrogant. It is far more important to treat people like people and computers like computers. Computers do not have feelings; they do not get happy or sad, they just run programs. In fact, very often in my career as an IT professional, I have let computers take the blame for things when I knew differently but also knew pointing it out would do nothing to solve the problem and leave people feeling unduly upset. I myself was of the type who preferred machines over people, and this is one of the reasons I went in to photography. I hated and still hate having my picture taken. So I could identify with the students, which I think was helpful in trying to make them better techs over all. I was not always completely successful and sometimes failed miserably with some students who were technically very good and just absolutely could not relate to regular people. I always hoped that I at least softened some of the edges some of them had.

The EET department got moved around a few times. We had started in Solberg Hall, which was not in very good shape and eventually the second and third floors got condemned. We ended up with some of our classrooms and offices including mine in Grove Hall, which had been a commons or place for students to eat and was converted to classrooms and offices, with most of our labs including the ones I used being in the basement of Hanson Hall which was a dorm on the other side of campus. This made for some pretty frantic trips from a class in Grove Hall to a lab in Hanson in the roughly 10 minutes I had between.

Eventually we were forced out of Grove by another department who for some reason had more power on campus than we did. We moved back into parts of Solberg, called the annex, or as I called it the sheep shed. My office was now attached to my classroom/lab which was convenient, but the space was frankly not very good: poorly lit, floors were far from flat (in fact wavy), poor ventilation, it was either way to hot or way to cold, not much of an in between. Eventually they rebuilt the main part of Solberg, including adding an elevator and an entrance with no steps. Our offices and labs were moved into this new completely renovated area. What they had done was leave the shell of the building and basically built another new building inside of it. My office was now only two down from where it had been when I was a GTA and my new classroom/lab was connected to my office. It was an ideal setting for teaching.

Solberg Hall as it is today. My original office was on the second floor over the main entrance, where there is sort of a balcony. It was the far left office in that group. After the renovation, my new office was the far right of the same area, and my classroom/lab connected to it is the room on the far right. The elevator and zero step entrance was added on the far left.

In the spring of 2011, South Dakota was in the midst of budgetary problems. The new governor decided to do an across the board 10% cut and when the budget finally came out in March, after the legislative session came to an end, we were called in for an emergency department meeting. The Dean of Engineering was there and announced that to meet the budget cuts for the College of Engineering he was going to eliminate the EET program along with the MNET program! We were shocked! As part of that cut, most of the personnel from those programs would be eliminated after two years. The two years were given so that the programs had time to funnel out the existing students. Personally, I felt I was in a good position to be one of the few that would be kept on, as I had the most seniority within not just the EET program but the whole department. He said he would meet with each of us individually the next day to tell us our status.

The following day he, along with my department head, came to my office, and once again I was shocked, as he informed me my job was being eliminated! He said he would guarantee me two years then I was done. He gave the usual, "I am sure it will all work out for you" and "you will land on both feet." I said, "You mean on all four wheels?" He laughed of course. I had already done some checking and found out that at the end of those two years I would still be a year and a few months away from meeting the magic Rule of 85. The Rule of 85 has to do with your time working for the state of SD under the retirement system and your age added together, with 85 being the result. When you hit the rule of 85 you could get full retirement benefits. I would be forced to take early retirement meaning since I would be at least 55, I would get retirement pay, but it would be hundreds of dollars less per month along with missing some other benefits. I didn't think it was fair, but life is not fair.

The following Monday morning, we had a group meeting with all the students in both programs. This meeting took place in my classroom since I already had the largest percentage of the students in my classes that day. After the department head gave the bad news and left, I gave my speech, which I felt was a defining moment in my teaching career. I gave the short version of what had happened at USD/S and I gave a strong speech about not letting this stop any of them from getting their degree, to not let the system beat them—to not be like the many students I knew from USD/S that just said screw it and went home never to return to college. I don't know if that changed a single person's mind, but I have to feel at least it helped them not give up. Even though I already knew I would almost certainly no longer have a full-time job there, I did everything I could to fire them up. I wanted to make sure they got through the system in the next two years and would be able to graduate with the full degree they had been seeking.

The next couple years were interesting and busy for me. That summer I taught a number of classes under one special topics listing. Special topics classes can be about anything and can be tailored to fit individual course needs and ones of this type can be used in place of any of the courses within our major as needed. This was to help students who had missed some classes that would not be taught again due to the closure of the program. I also did what I could to lobby anyone that would listen to me about the need for EET in South Dakota, including any legislators I knew who might care about this program. The following spring with the new legislative session and a very strong push by the founders of Daktronics, the Board of Regents announced the EET program would be reactivated, starting that fall, though changed to being ET instead of EET. I foolishly thought that meant I had my job back.

Since my position had been eliminated, I was told I would have to apply for the new job. It is possible to give preference to someone like me who had been at SDSU previously. I was not offered the job, but was told I could apply for it. I did apply when the position was officially announced that fall. I had all the required experience and my degree in EET was the exact one they were looking for, plus with my teaching degree and MSIM, I felt I had a decent chance. But it was not the case. They chose someone with a PhD in electrical engineering, which is not the same as electronic technology, but that is the way they went. I was more than a little disappointed that I had not even gotten an interview. I didn't think it was fair, but more than anyone, I know that life is not fair.

That fall I had a chance to teach electronic communications systems; I hadn't really taught it though that was my original major. I had always taught the computer classes instead. By that time I was the only one in the college that held an FCC license so it was quite appropriate that I teach it. I had a very large class, since anyone that had not taken it, had to then as it was the last time it would be offered. Since it had been long ago compressed from a full major to a single class there was a lot to cover in that class. It was great for me, as it allowed me to return to my roots a bit. I think I did a very good job and hoped the students got as much out it as I did. I honestly feel one of the real shortcomings of many techs in today's world is not having a good enough understanding of wireless type communications, both in the IT and in the cell phone world. Many are just technicians, simply installing systems with no real understanding of how they work. That works okay with wired communications, which is fairly cut and dried, but wireless is nothing like that. Unfortunately, now fewer techs in the future will have that type of instruction in the background.

One thing I have always done during my teaching and feel no need to apologize for is to err on the side of the student. I often got warned by administrators that I gave out too many A's. Perhaps so, but I felt that particularly in the higher level classes, most students have by then committed to the major and the less skilled or less committed students would have probably moved on to something else. There is a topic of discussion about grade inflation. As a teacher you get in more trouble by giving too many A's then you do for to many F's. If you give out too many A's you are not properly challenging the top students. In response, I think it is more important to pull up the middle and lower students, to teach towards them. The top students will most often excel on their own; the others might not. There have been a number of times in my teaching career where I have given a student a grade that arguably was better than they deserved, but that grade made a difference to them. They actually rose to meet the grade and in many cases, ended up as some of the best and most dedicated students. I determined to make sure that, as we filtered the last students out, I followed my true feelings on grades. If that meant more A's than the administration wanted, so be it.

I officially "resigned" my position and retired in May of 2013. I was later offered and accepted a part-time position to teach classes online in the fall, though not classes in the ET program. So I started teaching GE 109 freshman seminar, a special online only section for non-freshman and non-traditional students. Non-freshmen would be students who were returning to college after some time away, also those who for one reason or another hand not taken the course as freshmen. Non-traditional would be older students, many who had not gone to any college before. I also taught GE 231 "Technology, Society and Ethics." This class really helps the student see things from different perspectives, finding that more often than not, the best answer is in a compromised middle ground. I have had many students report back to me that the course changed not just how they thought about the topics, but how they thought about and viewed everything. I have taught one or both of these courses in the semesters since my official retirement. I like to teach and feel that with these classes I can continue to make a positive difference for the students.

Chapter 33

While in Brookings, I got closer to many of Tom and Rose's children, my cousins. Many of them attended SDSU over the years. I mostly got closer to Mary and Rita. They both worked for me when I had the retail store and would often hang out at my apartment and later my house. Mary really helped me a lot in starting up my computer store. She would stop by often with her son Shane, who was kind of my little buddy. Mary and her husband John lived in White while John finished at SDSU. He worked Friday nights so Mary and Shane would often come for supper and movies. Sunday evenings were their bowling nights and Shane would hang out with me. We always had a good time. I am pretty easy going with kids and would let him watch whatever he wanted on TV. The only time I really disciplined him was when he took my screw driver that I always kept in my pocket and he would "fix" things with it. This was fine until he thought he should "fix" the electric socket with it! I told him no a couple times and he thought it was funny. I finally grabbed him and spanked him after he got within an inch of putting it in. The only other time we had an issue was on Halloween one year. Mary had brought him to Brookings for some trick or treating. He was in his costume and he came running up to me. He yelled, "Trick or treat!" and kicked me in the knee! He didn't hurt me, but it was such a shocker! To this day I have no idea where that came from.

One time we had pizza which was fairly standard and often delivered by Pizza Pat (Patrick Bickett) from Pizza Hut. Anyway Shane ate three large pieces and was so funny, his tummy was as hard as a rock. Another time he found my coffee I had left over from morning (I drank magnum coffee at the time, from a pot, with a heaping teaspoon of instant coffee added in), and he ran around like crazy the rest of the night while as I recall Mary and I tried to work on her wedding stuff. Another time Mary had left him there while she and

John went bowling, and Shane wasn't feeling well. He woke up right after they left and spent most of the rest of the time on my lap crying "I want my mom." Another Saturday Mary had dropped him off at work just before I closed at noon, and I took him through McDonalds then home him sitting on my coffee table watching cartoons and eating fries with his ketchup ;) he would often dredge the same fry through ketchup and lick it off a number of times. Once he came for supper, I asked what he wanted. He said "beans and ketchup" and that is what he really wanted. A few years later at my house in Brookings, they were staying with me a few days. At the time Shane had an aversion to eating farm animals. I made chicken breasts with shake and bake. We didn't tell him what it was. He started eating and said "good perch," so we just let it go. ;)

Mary and Rita with their dogs, Cassy and Molly

When I turned 39, Mary and Rita thought I was turning 40 and when I got up in the morning and looked out the window at my Bronco, I saw it was all decorated with balloons and streamers. It was cute and pretty funny since I was only 39 at the time. On another birthday occasion of mine a couple years later, we met in Sioux Falls at Red Lobster. It was Mary and her girls Mariah and Katie, Pat and his wife Stacy and Rita. Rita, who was always thinking she needed to diet, yet she was as skinny as a rail, said she wouldn't order anything, but would just taste test what others were ordering and then she planned on ordering desserts. Well I think she eventually ordered every dessert on the menu and we all shared them. It was a really great time.

Lisa Schultz Carolin, Rita, and Sara Rogers
from that Christmas

One year Rita and her friends Lisa and Sara came to my apartment to decorate for Christmas. One of the best days ever! Rita, Lisa Schultz and Sarah Rogers came over to my apartment and we went and got a Christmas tree and decorations. Rita had decided that we were doing a "Red" theme. All the ornaments and lights were red. We even joked about getting a Red Angel for the top. We actually found one, but decided that would be a bit much. They all wore cute elf hats. We ended up shopping at Kmart, which is where we bought the tree. It was a fairly large very nice artificial tree, which I later gave to Rita when she moved into her and Jeff's first house in Harrisburg. After Kmart, we went to Pamida, which is where we found the Red Angel, but we decided on a white one instead. Finally to Walmart. It was one of the prettiest Christmas trees I ever saw once it was all decorated, and what a great time we all had putting it together.

When I had the retail store, as I mentioned, I would often take one of the workers along as my legs. One time it was Rita and I remember we went into a building and someone held the door for me. I went on to say that I hated it when people did that. At that time I walked with my crutches and braces and for someone that is good with crutches like me, where they are really an extension of your arms, holding doors is easy. Crutches actually make excellent door stops with their rubber tips. Rita said, "You are looking at it all wrong. Letting people do things like that for you makes them feel good about themselves for helping, so in fact you are doing them a favor by allowing them to help." Ever since then I have looked at things like that in a completely different way. I now just smile and say an honest thank you to them.

I eventually moved out the apartment and bought a double wide mobile home. Dennis and one of my students who had graduated moved most of my stuff and Mary and Rita helped me get it in order. It was pouring rain that day and we soon found there was a leak around my chimney. Rita asked her boyfriend Jeff, whom she would later marry, to stop over. He worked in roofing and came right over and in the pouring rain he fixed the leak. Jeff also built the deck on the back of my house and he also later updated it.

Tom and Rose's youngest son, Chris, was graduating from the Naval Academy in Annapolis, and all his family were making the trip out there, some as a road trip, some by plane. I ended up driving out with Mary, John and Shane in my car. I had a connection in the motel industry and being the planner I am, made all the plans and reservations. My connection was able to get us rooms pretty much everywhere we needed to stop for under $50, each which was a very good deal. Except for Canton, OH, John wanted to visit the Football Hall of Fame located there. I managed to get us fairly cheap rooms, for around $100, but when we got there they had mistakenly given our rooms away! They ended up setting us up for free in a nearby motel, which was at least as nice, so it worked out very well.

We went to the Football Hall of Fame the next day. It was mildly interesting, though for me about a half hour's worth, as I was not really into pro sports in any way. When we left we got turned around and lost for a bit but then made it the rest of the way to Arlington, VA. The next morning we were to meet a number of the Bicketts at the monuments area by the Whitehouse and the capitol buildings. John had talked to someone who said we should take the rail into as it would be impossible to get a decent parking space, I didn't really like that idea since it was my car and being handicapped I thought there had to be some decent parking we could use. And in any case we managed to miss the turn off to take the train in anyway. We had decent directions, but it got a bit chaotic. I was driving and we just kind of headed towards the Washington Monument. We managed to take all the correct turns and ended up in a parking lot next to the monument and guess what? There was a handicapped spot that was the absolutely closest you could possible park to the monument! We were the first ones of our group there and so started just kind of looking around. Tom and Rose called and were a bit lost but finally managed to get there, and went into the same parking lot and ended up parking only about a space down on the other side, so within 50 feet of each other! When they were getting of the car Mary's girls Katie and Mariah, who had come with Tom and Rose, said, "That's Marks car!" Tom at first thought they were crazy until he noticed it had South

Dakota plates starting with the number 6, which is Brookings County.

Of course it was interesting to see the monuments. The one that touched me the most by far was the Vietnam War Wall. To see the notes from loved ones stuck into the wall and at the base of it, really brought back the horror of that war. While we were touring members of the Bicketts took time pushing me around in my wheelchair. It was a great time, except when I went to jump off a curb that didn't have any sort of ramp. Dennis said "I got you." I popped a wheelie and jumped off the curb. Unfortunately he didn't quite have me, as I flipped over backwards, hitting the curb luckily not with my head, as Mary had but my camera bag on the handles of the chair. Plus, as soon as I knew I was going over I leaned forward as much as I could, so in the end I was not hurt in any way nor was the wheelchair or camera, though I never let Dennis live this one down. You see Dennis is a physical therapist by trade. Actually I know a very good one, but I have to give him a hard time when I get the chance anyway.

While there we visited a Museum of History. They had an exhibit of computer history. The thing that stuck out in my mind was they had an old original IBM PC and it looked much worse for wear. I actually at that time had one almost exactly like it, except mine was in much better shape and actually still worked, though even at that time it wasn't really of any use other than perhaps in the trunk of your car during the winter for weight—they are very heavy—or as a jack stand if you need to change your oil or something. Very sturdy construction, and of course if you ever needed a door held open they were good for that as well.

I didn't actually attend much of the graduation festivities, though we did go on a tour of the Academy, which was very interesting, including the lobby of the dorm which has about 10,000 steps to get into it and no elevator, so four of Mary's brothers each grabbed a point on my wheelchair and carried me up and later down.

On the way to DC, Mary's husband John and I had shared driving. It was fairly stressful for me to have anyone else driving my car, but it did work out ok a couple times as this was back before GPS was common on phones. I had directions from AAA maps as well as a decent atlas so when we were in places like DC I was navigator and that worked out. On the way home we headed out right after our tour of The Naval Academy and Annapolis and since I had pretty much just rested the two days after we got there, and others had partied much more, I ended up just driving the whole way back. We left Annapolis at about 1PM local time. I drove almost straight through until just after midnight when we crossed into Indiana and managed to find a hotel with rooms for the night. We were then up again at eight the next morning and again I drove the whole way. Luckily it was Sunday and the traffic was fairly light. We made it back to Brookings at about ten that night. I didn't even go any place, when we stopped and got gas, I either pumped gas or at least stood up a bit by the car to stretch some, and drank just the right amount of diet coke to not have to go to the bathroom. We pretty much just ate at the roadside plazas on the interstate, grabbing something on the go.

That same summer, Mary had a teachers conference in Grand Rapids Michigan. I went with just for something to do. I did some checking as I wasn't all that thrilled about going through Chicago again, not to mention the extra distance. Grand Rapids is almost straight east of here, but Lake Michigan is in the way. I found there was ferry that went across the lake from Manitowoc, WI to Ludington, MI. We decided to give it a try. I had calculated and the cost was almost awash with the cost of gas to go around. As it turned out we didn't get out of Brookings until fairly late that evening, and as we were driving I noticed my car was getting hot. We stopped for gas and I filled up the overflow reservoir and bought an extra gallon of antifreeze/coolant. Though it was in July, luckily it was at night. I kept an eye on it and even shut off the engine going downhill a few times. I managed to keep it from getting too hot. We stopped at some little town overnight, got a few hours of sleep then off again. Unfortunately it was Sunday and we couldn't find a place open, so I nursed it along until we got to the ferry landing. Luckily it had plenty of time to cool off and when we got to the other side, it was raining and only in like the 60s so we did make it to the hotel ok. I was very glad I had AAA. I called and they set me up with a local garage that did a great job fixed up and at a reasonable price. They also picked it up and delivered it back.

We had planned a fairly leisurely trip back, but the night before we were supposed to leave at about 10:30 I got a call on my cell from one of my service contract customers with a major problem with their QuickBooks and no backup, and payroll needed to be done. I told them to call QuickBooks in the morning. The next morning we headed to Ludington, MI and the ferry. That part was leisurely: as the ferry runs at certain times there was no reason to rush there. We even spent a little time by the beach on Lake Michigan. My customer had called QuickBooks and were told if they fed-exed the file to them they could probably repair it. Unfortunately no one at my customer's business could manage to copy the file.

The ferry got to the WI side about 11PM. We had planned to stay in a hotel there, but with the need to get back to Brookings we decided to drive through. I made it until we got into Minnesota about 3AM. Mary had slept since we got off the ferry so she was able to drive the rest of the way. We got to Brookings about 7AM, got 2 hours' sleep, then I went to my customers and copied the file for them. They ended up spending the whole day messing around and didn't actually get the package to Fed-ex until the next day. QuickBooks, true to their word, fixed the file and sent it back as soon the same day they got it. It did manage to work out as it barely got back in time for me to go to the business and restore the file before they had to get payroll out.

In the summer of 2003, I was thinking I needed a garage. It was getting harder for me to get around and the idea of being able to get in and out of my car without having to deal with snow covered steps was very appealing to me. By that time Rita and Jeff were married and Jeff was a contractor in Harrisburg, SD. I talked to Rita and together we came up with plans. I managed to get the bank to finance it so we were set to go. I really have to say, I don't know if this project would have come together without Rita's help. I have never been very good at asking for help, but I knew I could not really afford the garage if I had to pay labor as well as materials. Rita enlisted Jeff, of course, along with her brothers. Rita was always the type of person that no one could say no to. She had this wonderful way of making everyone feel like they were the most important person in the world. They came and built my garage over a couple of weekends. It is a well built garage, better than I could have gotten any other way. It has a ramp in it that is completely up to code and is excellent for me. The garage appears to be connected to the house, but it really isn't. Everything is done top notch. I thank them all every day in my mind, now that I am pretty much confined to a wheelchair. I really don't know how I could get along without my garage.

The fact that I ended up getting mostly confined to a wheelchair is in great part due to my own stubbornness. I had gotten to the point that walking was painful, in fact I was in pain most of the time; my "good" or right knee and ankle suffered the most, as well as my back and shoulders. I had to take a number of Aleve every day, just to function, then more at night to be able to sleep. One of the things with crutches is that you wear out the rubber crutch tips and for the high grade aluminum crutches like mine you need special tips with a steel washer in them. The normal ones you might see at say a pharmacy or something are designed for wooden crutches or canes and will only last a day or two on mine, and when they go out it is not fun.

I was in need of new tips, and found a place in Watertown that had them, so the next time I was by there, I decided to stop in. Well, they had very loose gravel in their parking lot and I slipped getting out of my car. Now normally my brace protects my left leg pretty good, but the way I fell, it actually ended a problem and something popped in my knee and hurt like hell. I had a hard time getting back up that was made worse by the pain and a couple kind-hearted but not very helpful people trying to help me up. I finally managed to get up and get in and buy the tips, but could barely stand the pain. I ended up going back home rather than up to see Mary as I had planned.

A couple days later, I was coming out of the bathroom babying my left leg and tripped, banging my right knee. I managed to get back up, but about an hour later, I could barely walk at all and finally not at all and had to call an ambulance to take me to ER. It turned out I had just broken a blood vessel in my knee, but until I could get into see an orthopedic doctor, they couldn't do much. And the soonest I could get an appointment was a couple days later. I ended up ordering a wheelchair off the internet and having to rent one until that showed up. I did still walk some for a few years after that, but it got harder and harder and finally I had to mostly give it up. Had I started using the wheelchair a few years earlier, I am pretty sure I could still walk some now. I am glad at least I can still stand up when I need to, to be able to get in and out my car and bed by myself.

In mid-October of 2004, Rita was diagnosed with leukemia. This was a very difficult time for all of us. Concerned family and friends had a benefit to raise funds to help with the medical costs the family faced. She did have decent insurance, but there are so many things that just don't get covered.

During this time I was talking to Rita and she said how she just hated asking people for help, and didn't like having all these people offering to help all the time. I said, "Rita, a very wise person once told me…" and then I reminded her of what she had told me about people holding the door for me. At that point I truly understood what she had meant back then. I wanted to do something, anything, to make it better for Rita. It wasn't possible to take away the pain, but at least you could do something to feel like you were helping in some small way.

She went through radiation and chemo. I went to see her as often as possible and made it my job to try and at least make her smile if not laugh every time. I almost always succeeded. Early on I gave her an envelope with some dollar bills and some change in it. I remembered as a kid being in the hospital and people would come to visit and there would be little things like a bottle of pop or a candy bar you wanted and had to pay cash for. This way, if someone came she would have some cash for such things.

They did a bone marrow transplant from her brother Chris, a big strong US Marine, and it seemed to go well. That following summer we were all at a lake in Minnesota camping. I really had a great time and I was able to spend a lot of time with Rita. She was a bit put out because she couldn't go swimming or really go in the water at all. We talked about not being able to participate in those activities and I think I was able to put things in good perspective for her. I talked about how we need to focus on the things we can do, not what we can't do. Rita's hair, which she had lost through chemo, was coming back and I remember her having me feel it. It was as soft as a baby kitten.

She continued with some treatments, although things seemed to be going quite well. In August that all changed. The cancer was back with a vengeance. She was told she had perhaps a couple weeks or maybe a little more to live on this earth. Rita and Jeff had two precious little girls, Autumn and Brooklyn. They decided that they should take a trip to Disneyland in California. Rita had always wanted to go there but never had been able to. She was hard to convince, even then, because she said it was just too expensive. We told her that some rich benefactor had donated the money for the trip, when in truth, we all donated whatever we could and they had a wonderful trip although by towards the end of it Rita was pretty tired. I am so glad they were able to make that trip.

During Rita's battle with cancer, some good friends of hers, Dawn and Kristin, were always there helping. They were a good part of organizing the benefit the year before and also for the trip to Disney.

I tried to visit Rita as often as possible. She was in a lot of pain, yet she made it so easy on me. She would always ask about what was going on in my life and work and if I had talked to one of our mutual friends who had worked for me as well, Jinny Struck. She'd ask how she was doing and how her kids were doing. I am so glad for all those times I went and saw Rita. When I couldn't get there, I tried to call. We worked it out, that I would call often at times when others were busy and if I did call and she was busy, then she would just tell me, or call me back if she felt like it when she wasn't busy. One thing she asked me to help with was a wish for her daughter. Autumn had always wanted to win this special Barbie they had at Chuck-e-Cheese. We had plans to go there for Mary's daughter Katie's birthday and she asked if I could find out if they would just sell the Barbie to me, but alas while they did sell stuff outright, they no longer had that Barbie. Now my computer skills were useful: I got on the internet which was much harder to find things on than it is now. I managed to track down the Barbie and get it to Rita without Autumn's knowledge.

Her brother Chris was getting married in the end of October and she really wanted to go to that wedding. The doctors had pretty much taken her off everything but painkillers at that point. They said that if they put her on fluids and some other things that maybe she could make it. But flying was out of the question, so Jeff managed to get the use of a very modern good motor-home and they made the trip. It went well and Rita came back appearing to be doing much better, like she was getting back to her old self. Even the doctors were surprised and they decided to get started on some other chemo drugs to see if it would help. She really seemed to be doing well. It was like a small miracle. We were talking often and I went to their house along with much of the family to celebrate Thanksgiving on I think the Friday or Saturday after Thanksgiving. That day she just seemed not to be feeling very well and just as I was getting ready to head home, she said she thought she needed to go to the hospital.

Things mostly went downhill from there. We talked a few times and she seemed to be doing fairly well, but then she was such a good actor. When you talked to her on the phone it was often hard to know how she was really feeling. On December sixteenth, I had called her and got the answering machine, when she called me back. We had a really nice chat. She was asking if I had all my Christmas shopping done and what I had gotten everyone. She seemed to be doing really well and I felt good about it, though it struck me as odd, when we were saying goodbye she said, "I Love you," when she would normally just say something like, "Talk to you later" as it turned out that was the last time I ever talked to her. She slipped into a coma the next day and died on December 23rd.

Chapter 34

The following February was Autumn's birthday and I had been invited to their house for the party. I almost didn't go because I was working on a network server upgrade and it was going slow, but then all of a sudden I got it figured out so I went. When they were opening presents, it turned out they had saved the Barbie that I had ordered off the internet for her birthday. When Autumn opened it, she had sweetest smile, and looked up toward heaven and said, "Thank you mommy." I am very glad I went and was able to witness that moment, knowing I had been part of making that happen.

That summer I was traveling with Mary to pick up one of her girls from a summer camp in Minnesota. The conversation turned to Rita, as it often did. We talked about how athletic she was as a runner and how she still wanted to get better at it and share a fun run together with Mary. Mary asked what I would think about organizing a commemorative run/walk in Rita's name. She wanted to call it the Run for Rita; it would be set up as a fundraiser to assist those battling cancer. I agreed and thought it was an excellent idea! We talked about it a lot and I said I would work on setting up a website. Mary, along with her sister Cathy and her mom, Rose, would be in charge of the main organizing and I would be mostly just a worker bee in the system.

I was happy to be able to help and especially to be able to use my computer skills. I had often thought about trying to create a website, but never really had specific reason that I wanted to create one for. By this time I had already closed my retail computer store and was about as busy as I wanted to be without doing something like creating a website for myself. I created a Run for Rita website. I had it up and running within a week. I had gone to Yahoo! for hosting and creation and it went fairly well, though it was a bit expensive. The fee was $75 to start then $25 hosting fee per month moving forward.

The idea of a charity event like this is to not spend any more of the funds than necessary on the preparations/administration and to save as much from the run's proceeds as possible to give to the cancer patients we were trying to help. I paid all the start up costs along with the per month charges. Later I ended up revamping it completely by purchasing the domain name WWW.RUN4RITA.ORG and making a webserver for hosting that site along with others out of used computer parts at my house to make a separate server computer just to be a webserver. I now have a main webserver and two backups running all the time.

The first year the run was a bit shaky; we were just learning. The run did raise an amount more than we had ever expected and as a result, we were able to help a number of families dealing with cancer. The idea behind the run was to give the money with no strings attached. It was not for cancer research, but to help the families. Maybe it was to pay the electric bill or the rent or mortgage or take a family trip. Whatever was needed, just something to help take a bit of the burden off those dealing with cancer. The run is also a time to get together in Rita's honor have some activities for kids, and a picnic and overall a good time.

It was at one of the runs that I happened to be talking with Rita's friend, Kristin Tuttle, who was now working at CCHS, where I had graduated in 1973. She mentioned that the following year was going to be CCHS's 60th Anniversary and that they were looking for former students to write stories about where are they now and thoughts of their years at CCHS. These would be published in *Reflections,* the school newsletter. She asked if I would be interested; I said, "Sure, why not?"

Through Kristin, I got in touch with Julie Gehm at CCHS. She did a phone interview with me and wrote a nice article for the spring edition of *Reflections*. That September Nancy Naeve from KSFY came from Sioux Falls to SDSU and did a story about me. It was filmed in my office and my classroom during my communications class. There were some delays in getting the story ready for air on the TV station. It finally aired on Oct. 24, 2012, which was National Polio Day! Neither of us knew that before, so it was interesting how it had worked out.

That next summer, I had a call from a reporter for the Argus Leader in Sioux Falls. Dr. Morrison had died and they had talked to Julie at CCHS and asked if she knew of any former students or someone of interest who could talk about his time there. Julie thought of me and so that was the reason for the Argus call. I felt privileged to be able to talk about him and share with the public what he was like and what it was like at CCHS. Later, Julie emailed me about someone from the March of Dimes who had contacted her about finding someone who had survived polio to speak at the 75th Anniversary of the March of Dimes Event to be held in October. Again, she thought of me and I told them she would be glad to do that. I was put in contact with Megan Colwell of the South Dakota Chapter of the March of Dimes and after we emailed back and forth she finally called me to talk about the possibility of me speaking at the event/banquet. After I accepted the invitation she, out of the blue, asked me about my connection to Run for Rita.

As part of my e-mail signature, I included a line that says: 'check out www.run4rita.org if you get a chance.' She had seen it there and was curious. I told her of my blood relationship as well as friendship with Rita and I explained that I had done all the computer/web site creation for it and also was the person who checked people in at the run. It turns out she was a friend of Rita's and also of her sister Cathy and that she had been to some of the runs! We had met and never realized it. What a small world it is.

I did the speech for the March of Dimes that year on their anniversary, October 24, which also happens to be National Polio Day. Mary went with me to help with maneuvering around the space and for moral support. It was held with an event called Chefs of Sioux Falls. I was told the food was good, but I could not focus on food at all. I was just a little bit apprehensive about this speech. It actually went very well and I did much better than I thought I would. I have had speaking opportunities in a classroom setting, but I had never really spoken at anything as big as this. I had talked to my mom the week before while preparing and I was able to get a lot of good information about how the March of Dimes had helped me through my younger years.

In January of 2014 I was coming back from a trip to Fargo with Mary for some shopping and lunch at Red Lobster. After I dropped Mary off at her home in Sisseton, I was doing some deep thinking about my life experiences. We had talked a little about CCHS and I got to thinking about having shrimp that day at Red Lobster and how I never was one of the shrimp eaters (board members) at CCHS, and why couldn't I be? I was a teacher; I understood about schools and learning, also some of business. Why couldn't I be on the board there? When I got home, I emailed Julie Gehm and mentioned it. She said, "Why didn't we think of that before?" and that she would pass the powerful suggestion along. As it turned out, it happened to be perfect timing! CCHS, now Children's Care Hospital and School, was currently in the process of merging with South Dakota Achieve and while they had a number of members for the new board, they were still short a couple. They wanted someone who had not been on either board before and also they were hoping for someone who was not a resident of Sioux Falls. It sounded like it was tailored for me.

I had been wanting to take a tour of CCHS to see what changes they had made along with the new name. Julie Gelm arranged for it to take place and at the same time. I would talk with Anne McFarland, the CEO of the new nonprofit created by the merger, Lifescape. Mary went with me for the tour and it proved to be very interesting. There indeed were some changes there and yet much of it was still the same. The building had gone through many updates, but yet it was all so familiar and it also brought back all kinds of memories. The swimming pool, my favorite place, is almost exactly as I remembered it. I visited with Anne and she said she would put my name up to be elected to the board, although it would not be official until the May board meeting

After I was elected to the board at the May meeting, I have had the honor of serving on the board. It is so different seeing things from this completely different perspective. Even though they no longer have fried shrimp at the meetings, it has been a real eye opener. From the first meeting, where I had thought I would just sit and listen, but ended up participating, I have known it was a good choice. During the merger there were some IT computer issues, not that I had any hands on with that. I understood exactly what they were going through and had worked with the programs they had issues with and I think was able to explain why there were problems.

In February of 2015, we met in the South Dakota capital city of Pierre. Mary again went along with me as it was an overnight trip and just easier if I have a helper along. During our time in Pierre, we had a social with the Legislators at which time we were trying to get them to be on our side with issues that would affect Lifescape. At this social, I spoke with a number of people about Lifescape and stepped out of my comfort zone some to talk about how I had graduated from CCHS and my current connection. When I got back from Pierre I got to thinking about it all and that is what has led to this book.

What have I learned from all of this? First and foremost, you have to make the best of what you have. What you do in spite of—in fact, because of—a disability is the important thing. My polio is part of what led me to be better with computers; in an odd way it gave me an edge. Many of the skills I needed to survive with my disability are exactly what made me better with computers. I also learned to not look for someone or something to blame situations on because sometimes things just happen. We need to deal with it and move on. It is in our human nature to be the best we can be, to go as far as we can with what we have. We are all different. We each have our limitations and sometimes they are not obvious. We need to make sure that we do not let our limitations stop us from being all we can be, yet at the same time, we must recognize them and set our goals appropriately.

I have spent my whole life trying to get away from that poor little crippled kid, though as it turns out that has always been a great part of who I am. A great part of what has driven me to make the most of what I had, to be what I have become.

Epilogue

After writing and publishing the first edition of *Normal for Me*, I found that many people were asking for more, which frankly astounded me. I purposely kept the first edition short for a couple reasons; mainly, since I self published, every additional page costs money and I was trying to keep costs down as much as possible, since I had no idea how well the book would be received. The main reason was because I didn't want it to be boring. I didn't want it to be one of those books that as you read it, you keep thinking, "Isn't this thing over yet?"

I was a bit surprised how well the book was received, and also that it seems to have become more of a banner for vaccination that I had thought it would. While I am a strong advocate for vaccination and that was in great part where I found the motivation to write the book in the first place, it is only really mentioned in the first paragraph of the book.

On International Polio Day October 24th, 2015, my brother Jim and I went back to my home town of Scotland, SD for my first book signing at the public library. I was overwhelmed with how well it went. I ended up selling 45 copies of my book, spoke to many people, a lot of old friends as well as many I did not know. We also took some time to drive around town and check things out—many things had changed, many things had not. All and all it was a very good day.

Whenever I am asked to speak about my book and my life I do mention vaccination in the strongest terms. I like to point out, while holding up a copy of my book, that my mom has felt a fair amount of guilt about what happened to me, I always tell her, "Mom, there is not a darn thing you could have done differently, it is what it is." When I speak, I then go on to say suppose you purposely choose to not vaccinate your child for whatever reason and your child ended up with polio, ended up like the child on the cover of my book, how would you possibly live with yourself?

I have spoken to groups from freshmen in high school through graduate school, as well as to many civic organizations. I have been very honored at how well I have been received in all cases. One of the first times I spoke was to students in a graduate class at SDSU. I found out that one of the students went home and told her roommate, "It was the best class ever!" I never had that sort of response when I taught full time in the classroom and it was very gratifying.

At the January 2016 board meeting of Lifescape I happened to mention to Dr. Billion that I wish I could afford to give every legislator in South Dakota a copy of my book. I had looked into it but it was way to expensive for me to handle. He said immediately, "That is a great idea! I will fund it!" I said that I would offer him a deal: books at cost. He would hear nothing of that, said he would pay full price. In the end he and another board member Henry "Chip" Carlson purchased the required copies of the book and we gave them to the legislators when we had the Lifescape Social in February 2016.

I had been trying to contact the governor's office to get a meeting to present a copy in person to the governor. When I got home from that January meeting there was a message waiting on my answering machine that said, "Sorry but the governor doesn't have time on the date you specified." They did leave a number which I called back and pleaded my case for why I thought my book and myself were worthy of taking even a few minutes of the governor's busy time. The lady was nice but said she doubted there was anything that could be done, but that she would pass along my request. Someone from the office called me back the following Monday and after some more badgering on my part I was able to secure a time to meet with the governor for a few minutes to present my book on the same day as the social was to be in February.

Henry 'Chip' Carlson and I meeting with and presenting a copy of my book to South Dakota Governor Dennis Duagaard

The meeting with the governor went very well, as did the Lifescape Social. I met and spoke with a number of legislators, including one I had really wanted to meet: Senator Billie Sutton of Burke, South Dakota. I even had one legislator ask if I could possible come back later in the session when her committee was talking about vaccination, I had to decline, but it was nice to get the offer.

Please vaccinate your children.

Oh, and still no fried shrimp at the board meetings.